Parent Engagement in Early Learning

Parent Engagement in Early Learning

Strategies for Working with Families

Second Edition

JULIE POWERS

www.redleafpress.org
800-423-8309

Published by Redleaf Press
10 Yorkton Court
St. Paul, MN 55117
www.redleafpress.org

The first edition of this book was published in 2005 as *Parent-Friendly Early Learning: Tips and Strategies for Working Well with Families.*

Second edition 2016
Cover design by Elizabeth Berry
Cover photographs by Getty Images/XIXINXING
Interior design by Percolator
Typeset in Karmina and Karmina Sans
Printed in the United States of America
23 22 21 20 19 18 17 16 1 2 3 4 5 6 7 8

Library of Congress Cataloging-in-Publication Data

Names: Powers, Julie, 1957– author.
Title: Parent engagement in early learning : strategies for working with families / Julie Powers.
Other titles: Parent-friendly early learning.
Description: Second edition. | St. Paul, MN : Redleaf Press, [2016] | Previous edition: Parent-friendly early learning. 2005. | Includes bibliographical references.
Identifiers: LCCN 2015027614| ISBN 9781605544380 (pbk. : acid-free paper) | ISBN 9781605544397 (ebook)
Subjects: LCSH: Early childhood education—Parent participation. | Parent-teacher relationships.
Classification: LCC LB1139.35.P37 P693 2016 | DDC 372.21—dc23
LC record available at http://lccn.loc.gov/2015027614

Printed on acid-free paper

For Marty Rosenthal, who encouraged and supported me through completion of this book;

Gabriel Powers, who was patient while I learned how to be a parent;

Maggie Bryson, one of the best teachers we ever lost;

and Kathy Kolb, who understood my intent and helped me find the book inside me.

Contents

ix Acknowledgments

1 Introduction

---

11 Chapter 1: Developing Relationships with Families

20 *Scenario 1:* "What Is Going On at School?," or Building Trust

25 *Scenario 2:* Fear of Men, Strangers, and Dangerous Persons, or The Boogeyman

28 *Scenario 3:* The Parent Who Drains You, or "Excuse me, but I have some children here who need my attention."

---

33 Chapter 2: Communicating with Families

46 *Scenario 4:* Recommending a Child for Assessment, or "What is wrong with Tim?"

51 *Scenario 5:* When Parents Don't Read Your Newsletters, or "Why didn't you tell me she has a field trip today?"

---

57 Chapter 3: Policies That Work for Families and Staff

66 *Scenario 6:* Parents Who Don't Follow School Rules, or "But we're special!"

71 *Scenario 7:* Fear of Health Problems Part 1, or The Sun Devil

76 *Scenario 8:* Fear of Health Problems Part 2, or Typhoid Mary

81 *Scenario 9:* The Parent Who Won't Leave, or "How can I miss you when you won't say good-bye?"

88 *Scenario 10:* The Late Parent, or "Is it 6:15 already?"

92 *Scenario 11:* The Parent Who Wants Special Treatment, or "If it's not too much trouble . . ."

96 *Scenario 12:* The Child with Special Needs, or "Why didn't you tell us?"

101 Chapter 4: Finding Common Values between Home and School

106 *Scenario 13:* When Beliefs from Home and the Program Don't Match, or Holidaze

111 *Scenario 14:* Controlling Pretend Play, or "Not my son!"

115 *Scenario 15:* Fear of Losing Influence over One's Own Child, or "Whose child is this, anyway?"

120 *Scenario 16:* Separating Twins, or "Why can't my boys be together?"

---

125 Chapter 5: Child Development Issues

130 *Scenario 17:* Taking School Toys Home, or "My little Jesse James"

134 *Scenario 18:* The Parent Who Personalizes Her Child's Rejection, or "Then you can't come to my birthday party."

139 *Scenario 19:* The New School Year, or "Where are my daughter's friends?"

144 *Scenario 20:* The Child Who Can Do No Wrong, or "Not my baby!"

---

149 Chapter 6: Involving Your Director to Work Well with Families

159 *Scenario 21:* Not Really Toilet Trained, or "Oops! Not again!"

164 *Scenario 22:* When a Child Reports an Event to Parents Incorrectly, or "I want to talk to the parents about what really happened!"

---

171 Checklist for Analyzing Scenarios

173 References and Recommended Readings

Acknowledgments for Second Edition

Thanks to Kara Lomen for making this second edition the best it could be with her wonderful editing. Thanks to Sherry Nolte for her gentle and helpful editing and Jennifer Ikehara, Michelle Tancayo, Alexandra Domingo, Tamika Smiley, and other University of Hawaii Maui College students for sharing their stories of working with families

Acknowledgments for First Edition

Thanks to the following:

- Marjorie Schiller, who always thinks I am smarter than I am
- Eva Moravcik, who trusted my ego with her mighty red pen and made improvements to this book
- Roger and Bonnie Neugebauer, who believed I had something to say to my colleagues
- Stephanie Feeney, who taught me how to think about professional ethics
- Margarita Kay, who taught me to look at cultural context
- Betty Jones, who pushed me to improve my writing
- Nancy Burrows, who modeled the role teachers can play in improving parents' competency
- Kay Rencken, who helped me find my professional voice
- Nancy Sergeant-Abbate, who taught me how to collaborate with parents
- Beth Wallace, who stepped in at the eleventh hour and saw to it that this book was the best it could be
- Marcie Oltman, Jenny Hanlon, Natalie Dube, Louie Kolberg, Sarah Sivright, Sheila Williams-Ridge, Kathy Zampier, Susan Knutson, Joel Creswell, Jacky Turchick, Rheta Kuwahara, Cheryl Takashige, and Doug Rowe, for sharing their stories of working with families
- All of the families of University of Hawaii at Manoa Children's Center, Dodge Nature Preschool, Valley View Preschool, and Tucson Community School for sharing their children with me

Introduction

Have you ever worked with a teacher who thrives on working with parents? For some teachers, relationships with parents are as fulfilling as relationships with children. Rather than stressing out before parent-teacher conferences, these teachers look forward to the time they will spend talking with parents about the children. Parents seem to listen to their advice and trust them with family issues. These teachers are even able to tell parents hard truths without being met with defensiveness. Are they just natural parent educators? Some may be. Others may have once been uncomfortable working with parents, but as they gained the skills to build relationships with parents, they learned to enjoy this aspect of their work. If you find working with parents one of the more difficult aspects of your job, you are not alone. This book will help you understand how teachers develop natural relationships with parents and teach you the skills you need to enjoy your work with parents too.

But am I talking about parents, or am I talking about families? I call this book *Parent Engagement in Early Learning* because in it I am talking about parenting. Parenting is done by many members of a child's community. For some children, grandparents, aunts, family friends, and others take on the parenting role. In this book, I use the terms *parents* and *families* somewhat interchangeably. When I do, I am referring to all the people who assume the role of parenting a young child.

When I was a young teacher working in a parent-cooperative nursery school, I called a mentor who had worked in another parent co-op for many years. I described the unreasonable expectations of the parents I was working with ("My child can sit still for an hour in church; I don't see why you aren't having her sit still and learn at school"), their lack of follow-through (parents forgetting to bring snack on their day or not staying to clean up after their day in the classroom), and their general lack of respect for my knowledge. My friend said to me, "It helps when you are old enough to be the parent's mother." "I'm not willing to wait that long!" I blurted out.

It didn't take that long. The more confident I became in my knowledge, the more the parents respected me. The surer I was that my expectations of parents were reasonable, the more they followed through on those expectations. Most importantly, the more I relaxed and allowed myself to enjoy these people, the better my relationships with them grew. I can now say that my work with parents has been one of the most enjoyable parts of my career in early childhood education.

One of the keys to working well with parents is learning to see their perspectives. As teachers, we can appreciate children for who they are and take pleasure in their company when we understand their development and their unique way of looking at the world. We enjoy some children more than others, even if we pretend we like them all the same, but as teachers we know how to make relationships with all children. The same can be true of our relationships with parents. Parents are unique individuals, and we will enjoy some more than others, but we can create relationships with all of them. Sometimes the parents who are challenging end up being the parents we feel the closest bond to. Working well with parents makes teaching more satisfying.

Why Is It Important for Us to Work with Families?

Sometimes we see the need to work well with parents as just one more demand on teachers. Aren't children the most important focus of our work? Why should we dilute our efforts and focus on parents as well?

Because it's the best thing for children. Working with families is important because, simply put, it's the best thing for the children. Children gain the most from their early education experience when a partnership exists between teachers and families. When we, as teachers, have a positive impact on the whole family and affect how they interact with their children, we make a contribution that will last a lifetime.

Because we have a lot to offer parents. As early childhood education (ECE) professionals, we have special insight into the needs and interests of young children. When we work with parents, we can help them differentiate between issues that are related to general development and issues that are specific to their children. We can help them keep their expectations age appropriate and offer families solutions to struggles they may be having with their children.

Because parents have a lot to offer us. We need to work with families because parents know their children well—and they can help us find the strategies to best teach their children. They know their children's preferences and abilities and are able to read their children's feelings. Our jobs will be easier in partnership with parents.

Why Do Some Teachers Find It So Hard to Work with Parents?

Talking to parents can practically paralyze some teachers. As one preschool teacher said, "I just dread parent-teacher conferences! I get so nervous—all of my thoughts just leave my brain! Sometimes parents get defensive if I tell them anything less than glowing about their children." Communicating with parents can be especially hard for new teachers. Parents may not demonstrate patience with the learning curve for novice teachers. Anxious parents may cross-examine teachers or hover to make sure everything is okay. Building confidence is hard when you feel yourself being constantly critiqued.

Sometimes there is a cultural or economic divide between parents and teachers. I spoke to one teacher who moved from working with Head Start to a private, upper-income school. She said, "When I was in Head Start, the parents appreciated everything I did and treated me like a professional. Now I have these parents who expect me to wait on them and meet their personal needs. They treat me like I am a servant!"

Sometimes teachers struggle if they are not parents themselves. They may have difficulty relating to the lives and concerns of parents. These teachers may feel defensive about their judgment and advice to parents. Sometimes parents express a lack of confidence in the knowledge of a teacher who hasn't walked in their "parent" shoes.

Some early childhood teachers just relate to and interact better with children than with adults. Some of the traits that make a great early childhood educator—such as finding the behavior and personalities of children inherently interesting or having a talent for staying in the background rather than being the center of attention—do not translate to socializing well with adults.

How Can We Learn to Love Working with Families?

Most of us have what it takes to be good at working with parents. The characteristics that make us good with children can also serve us in our work with parents:

- We know how to facilitate learning.
- We appreciate individual differences.

- We focus on development.
- We are warm and caring.
- We are willing to give others the benefit of the doubt.
- We enjoy the development of competency.
- We develop warm relationships.
- We can make a difference.

We know how to facilitate learning. Teachers know how to create learning opportunities that allow children to construct their own knowledge by finding solutions to what frustrates or interests them. We can do that with families as well. We can pick up on the subtle cues of individual parents to tell us when they are ready to find answers to what frustrates them in parenting. When we know what each and every parent needs, we can guide them toward finding solutions that work for their own families. Our classrooms are laboratories for learning about children. When we share our insights and experiences with parents, and when we invite them into our classroom world, we can help them learn about their children.

We appreciate individual differences. When children join our classrooms, we accept them no matter where they are developmentally, and we celebrate their quirky and unique personalities. If we can find room in our hearts to also appreciate parents as individuals, they will enrich our lives. We can include their special talents and skills when we invite them into our classrooms. We can enjoy their senses of humor, be awed by their insights, and learn from them as people.

We focus on development. Teachers can use these same skills while we work with parents. We can work with a mother who is a genius in her own field but can't quite get herself and her child organized in the morning, as well as the father who is wonderful with his child but hasn't developed self-confidence in the decisions he makes as a parent. We can see that both of these people are still developing as parents. By paying attention to the development of parents, we can have reasonable expectations and not be disappointed when all of them don't make the choices we'd like them to make.

We are warm and caring. As teachers, we tend to be warm people who are comfortable with our own emotions as well as the feelings of others. This characteristic helps us work well with parents who may be experiencing a merry-go-round of emotions while they learn how to parent.

We are willing to give others the benefit of the doubt. We tend to be positive and optimistic people. We expect that even children who are struggling are going to turn out okay. We can use that optimism to anticipate the best in the parents we work with. We can enjoy parents. Some of the aspects we love most about working with children can also be present when working with families.

We enjoy the development of competency. We can tap into the joy of a parent's discovery in the same way we feel joy the first time a child pumps on a swing or writes her name. Watching a parent offer his child a choice rather than getting mad at him or overhearing one parent describe making it through a difficult stage of her child's development can be very gratifying.

We develop warm relationships. As teachers, we appreciate the affection children have for us, and we grow very fond of them. Some of us cry when children leave our programs. We can also enjoy very special relationships with parents. We share a wonderful time in the lives of their children. We are a quiet fan club for each child, noticing growth and achievements together. The relationships we develop with parents, whether professional or informal, can be a source of great enjoyment. As a program director, I loved to listen to easy laughter coming from parents and teachers at conferences while they enjoyed their shared wisdom about a particular child.

We can make a difference. We are not a cynical group. When Sue Bredekamp gave the closing keynote speech at the 2003 National Association for the Education of Young Children (NAEYC) Conference in Chicago, she described the culture of early childhood educators and how it prepares us to enjoy our work with families. One of the most relevant aspects of our ECE culture is our belief that we make the world a better place through our work. When we collaborate with parents to meet the needs of the children we serve, our energies and commitment have an even bigger effect on families and children.

Are You Ready to Develop Partnerships with Parents?

Attitudes and beliefs play a strong role in our ability to create partnerships. Take the following quiz to determine your own readiness.

1. Most parents want what is best for their children.
   ○ True ○ Somewhat true ○ Not true
2. If parents don't agree with me, one of us does not have to be wrong.
   ○ True ○ Somewhat true ○ Not true
3. Children benefit from communication and collaboration between their parents and teachers.
   ○ True ○ Somewhat true ○ Not true
4. My job is more enjoyable because of my interactions with parents.
   ○ True ○ Somewhat true ○ Not true
5. Parents can offer me insight about their children that will help me do a better job.
   ○ True ○ Somewhat true ○ Not true
6. I can think beyond my own preferences and convenience to benefit children and parents.
   ○ True ○ Somewhat true ○ Not true
7. Parents are entitled to the final say in their children's care and education.
   ○ True ○ Somewhat true ○ Not true
8. I am willing to change routines and practices if doing so works better for children and parents.
   ○ True ○ Somewhat true ○ Not true
9. I grow as a professional through interaction with parents.
   ○ True ○ Somewhat true ○ Not true

How did you do? Your reactions to these questions can reveal some of your feelings that may help or hinder your relationships with parents.

If you answered "True" to most questions, you understand the value of parent-teacher partnerships and are ready to get better at them.

If you answered "Somewhat true" to most questions, you demonstrate interest in creating partnerships with parents but often keep your conflicting attitudes in mind. As you find yourself reacting negatively to parents' actions, push yourself to think from their perspectives.

If you answered "Not true" to most questions, you may have attitudes and beliefs that will interfere with building partnerships. Viewing parents as adversaries, problems, or a waste of your time will hold you back from improving your interactions with parents. As you read the following chapters, listen to the voices of parents and see if you can shift your thinking.

Does This Get Any Easier?

Working with parents may not be easy, but it's worth the effort—and yes, it does get easier. This book was written to help bridge the differences in perspective between early childhood teachers and parents. Each chapter provides a framework for thinking through the challenges of creating a family-friendly program—challenges such as developing relationships with families (chapter 1); communicating with families (chapter 2); developing family-and-staff-friendly program policies (chapter 3); developing parent-friendly program values (chapter 4); working with parents on child development issues (chapter 5), and working with your director to build and improve family relationships (chapter 6). Within each chapter, I present

- hypothetical problems from both teachers' and parents' perspectives,
- ways to create a climate of partnership while preparing to address these problems,
- suggestions for what to do (or not do) if the problem being illustrated comes up for you, and
- ways you can take your problem solving a step further to prevent similar issues in the future.

At the end of the book, I provide a checklist to help you analyze the challenges that surface in your work with parents (see page 171).

And who am I to give you advice about working with parents? I am like you. I have taught in many kinds of programs, including Head Start, part-day nursery schools, and full-day programs. When I taught in a parent-cooperative program, I became so frustrated trying to work with parents that I returned to graduate school to learn more about parent education and leadership. I eventually earned a master's degree from Pacific Oaks College with specialization in both early childhood education and parent/community work. I have since worked as a director and teacher in programs with many kinds of parents—parents of children with special needs, international parents, parents who are college students, and suburban parents—and have sought to develop authentic working relationships with families and to support teachers as they work with parents. I now teach full-time at University of Hawaii Maui College, and in every course I teach, I hear about the joys and challenges teachers face collaborating with families. It is my hope that this book provides you with insight into how to improve your daily interactions with families.

This New Edition

I have updated this book in response to the teachers and college students who have used the first edition and provided me with feedback. Thank you all! I've updated the book's information to reflect changes in families and in programs for young children over the past ten years. I have added two new chapters: communicating with families (chapter 2) and working with your program director on family issues (chapter 6). The chapter on relationships now includes information on parent-teacher relationships with special complications.

Within each of the chapters, I have added new scenarios based on challenges readers have shared, and I have included more information for the novice teacher. These example scenarios can be used in several ways. Novice teachers or teachers who are working with a new group of parents can use them to think about situations they may encounter from the parents' perspectives. Taking a proactive look at challenges can help prepare the ECE professional to avoid common pitfalls that may have a negative impact on relationships. Early childhood education students or workshop participants can also use these scenarios as ways to imagine how the theory they are learning in class can be put into practice. Finally, experienced teachers who are frustrated or experiencing challenges with parents can look for a similar situation in order to find new solutions to conflicts.

Finally, I have included a worksheet for examining challenges in working with families (see page 171). I have designed this worksheet as a tool to help you think about your own challenges, for trainers to use in workshops on working with parents, and for college instructors to use with their classes.

I hope this book has been useful as you work to improve your collaboration with parents. When you are able to enjoy working with families as well as with their children, you will be sustained in our field for years to come.

Developing Relationships with Families

The early childhood education field places a lot of stock in developing relationships between teachers and children. When programs are applying for accreditation, the "Standard 7: Families" section of the National Association for the Education of Young Children (NAEYC) accreditation is heavily weighted in importance. Enrolling children, orientation, style of interaction, scheduling—all are done with an eye on how relationships between children and teachers are built or hindered. If we believe that relationships between teachers and parents are critical to children's experiences, we must also work on developing these bonds.

Strategies for Developing Relationships

You can take a number of steps to develop positive relationships with families. Examine the list below to see if you are already taking these steps or if there are some you could add to your toolbox of strategies.

1. Take time to develop lasting relationships with parents.
2. Be available.
3. Be yourself.
4. Share while staying within your own personal boundaries.
5. Be trustworthy.
6. Remember that the relationship is in service to the child, not your needs.

Take time to develop lasting relationships with parents. One mom describes her feelings for the teacher:

> *"My daughter loves her teacher, but that's not the only reason I am crazy about Terry. She's just a neat person! She really seems to care about me as well as Tiffany. She asks about my day, notices my mood, and shares funny stories about her own child. I feel so lucky to have Terry in our lives."*

It sounds simple, but it takes time and commitment. Think of the steps you take to build a relationship with a new child in your program. You approach her cautiously, giving her time to get used to your presence. You try to pick up cues from her and adjust your own behavior to be inviting without being overwhelming. You give her time to trust you. You demonstrate yourself to be likable. You give her time to figure out that you are here to stay. You hope that you get a chance to have positive interactions with her before you have to set a limit or confront a negative situation.

The same is true of relationships with parents. Acknowledge that they are individuals just as their children are. Some are extroverted or will be easy to interact with. Others will take more time. Some will trust you instantly, and others will need you to prove yourself. Treat your developing relationships with parents as deliberately and as individually as you do with children. Don't expect the same actions (a friendly greeting or small talk) to be received in the same way by all parents. Reflect on a budding relationship, just as you do with children, and plan the next action with the understanding that a single formula won't work for all.

You know how to create relationships with children, but how do you go about it with adults? Here are five fundamental ways to lay the groundwork.

Be available. This doesn't mean chatting with parents when the children need your attention or staying after work for thirty minutes talking about a parent's new job. Instead, find a way to communicate with parents that works for both of you. This may be a quick conversation at the beginning of the day, phone calls in the evening, texts, or e-mail. If parents find you easy to talk to about little things, it will be easier for them to talk to you about difficult topics.

Be yourself. Sometimes parents idealize their child's teacher. You seem to have all the answers. Their child doesn't misbehave with you as he does at home. But a pedestal is a difficult place from which to build a relationship. Don't be afraid to show your faults. It is not useful for parents to think you are perfect.

Share while staying within your own personal boundaries. Teachers vary in their need for space from parents. You can still keep the amount of space you need while developing relationships with them. You do not need to be friends with the parents of the children you work with. It is also not inherently wrong to be friends with parents of the children in your class. There is no one right way.

Most parents respond positively to clear expectations from teachers. Some teachers are comfortable with more formal relationships—parents call them by their surnames, and teachers keep personal information private. Other teachers may develop easy intimacy with families—they openly share information about their own families and lives outside of school. If the openness is sincere, many parents will respond. Parents may be more forthcoming about their own children's difficulties if they know the teacher has had similar battles.

Be trustworthy. What may seem like a small thing to you may feel like a betrayal of confidence to a parent. Always ask if information is public (for example, moving, making a major purchase, taking a new job, having a medical condition, or becoming engaged). If parents ask you for casual information about another parent, be clear and friendly in your refusal to give information. For example, if a parent asks you if another child's parent is pregnant, you can answer by saying, "I really can't talk about families, but you are welcome to ask her mom when she comes for pickup." While the parent may be momentarily embarrassed, she will remember that you were trustworthy.

Remember that the relationship is in service to the child, not your needs. Friendships with parents are tricky, especially during the time the child is in your care. Enter these relationships with caution. The child can easily get pushed out of the way while the adults are enjoying each other. Sometimes we need to tell parents hard truths, and our personal relationships with parents should not get in the way.

Complicated Relationships

It is easier to develop relationships with some families than it is with others. Below, you will find examples of complicated relationships, suggestions of ways some teachers worked with these challenges, and tips that may help guide you in similar situations.

Complication 1: Highly Vulnerable Parents

While appropriate boundaries are important, sometimes we are the only people who see isolated parents on a regular basis. We may be in a situation where we can literally save their lives. We could be the ones who see mothers who are experiencing domestic violence and may be the only ones to get them help. Mental illness can fall into this category as well.

A teacher describes:

> *"Joannie's mom didn't look right when she dropped Joannie off at our Head Start classroom. She had obviously been crying for a long time. I asked her, 'Lani, are you okay?' She kept her head down. I put my arm around her and asked again. 'Eh, it's just no good,' she said, 'I'm no good. The kids be better off without me. I think I don't want to live no more. You take care of my Joannie for me, yeah?' She started to leave, and I said, 'Lani, you aren't going home. Today you stay and play with us. Joannie wants you to play with us today.' It took Lani awhile to settle in, but she did stay and play with us. The kids seemed to sense that she needed to be there and were so kind to her! When she was busy with Duck, Duck, Goose, I slipped away and called our family case manager. The case manager came right up and spent a long time with Lani. That was two years ago. Lani got the help she needed, and she is doing great."*

Tips for working with highly vulnerable parents:

- Know your resources. You won't have time to do research once these needs become visible.
- Come up with a proactive plan for parents who may need more. It is important to maintain confidentiality, but there are times when other staff members may need to step in.

Make sure that vulnerable parents know you see them as individuals and as more than their problems. Most interactions should still be about their child and their parenting rather than focusing only on their personal problems.

Complication 2: When Parents Didn't Choose Your Program

It is more challenging to develop relationships with parents who didn't choose your program. There are a number of reasons this may happen.

Listen to this divorced father:

> *"I don't know why Kathy's mother picked this program. I guess because her sister's kid goes there. All they do is play. I want her to go to a school where she actually learns something."*

Sometimes parents are forced to enroll their child in a program to receive subsidies:

> *"I don't even like this place. My older daughter went to a better school, but they aren't accredited, so I couldn't get the state subsidy to pay for it. If I can just get a raise at work, I'll be able to move her to that better school."*

The most challenging can be court-ordered placement:

> *"The only way I could get custody back for the twins was to enroll them in this school. I don't see why they can't just be home with me."*

Tips for developing relationships with parents who did not choose your program:

Go the extra mile to build these relationships. It is natural to feel hurt if parents don't cover up their lack of support for your program. Rather than writing them off, try harder to develop those relationships.

If you find a divorced couple has one parent who likes the program and the other doesn't, resist the urge to give more time, attention, and information to the friendly parent. You are only supporting the assumptions of the other parent when you behave poorly toward him or her.

Help parents who do not see the value of your program. Guide parents to understand why you do what you do. The trick is to do this without sounding condescending.

Recognize when your relationship has turned the corner with resistant parents. Just make sure not to say something that makes them lose face again, such as, "See, you didn't think we were such a great school, but now you see we were right!"

Complication 3: When the Parent Is On Staff

This is challenging for both the parent and the other staff. A teacher describes:

> *"The director has her kid in my class. All the rules go out the window! Whenever I try to discipline her daughter, she just runs to Mommy. The director lets her daughter just hang out with her. I have no authority with this child!"*

In this circumstance, it might be best to find out how the director wants you to handle disciplining her child. Look at the next chapter for ideas on how best to communicate the issue.

Being a parent who is also a teacher in the school can be hard. Sometimes you feel as if your child gets less time or attention than the other children because the staff expects you to understand. A parent-teacher describes:

> *"My son is in the two-year-old room, and the teachers help all of the other children when they need help on the toilet. When my son has to go number two, they just bring him to my classroom! I know they are really busy, but doesn't my son deserve as much care as the other children?"*

Tips for navigating parents who are staff members:

Begin with the expectation that policies for families will be consistent, even with parents who work in the center. You can make exceptions, but be overt about those exceptions, stating them and agreeing to them.

Have the parent-teachers keep their children in their own classrooms until the time when other parents would be allowed to drop off their children. Do not let staff children hang out in your classroom before school begins. This will avoid confusion for the children. It will provide a consistent message to all parents in your class regarding appropriate drop-off time. The other potential problem is you won't be able to accomplish much if a child is in the room with you outside of classroom hours. If you are trying to leave the room to gather supplies, leave cupboards open, or work with items that aren't child-safe, you won't get your work done and you'll be frustrated by unmet expectations. Instead, set consistent policies about when children can join your room. (See chapter 3 for more suggestions about setting policies.)

Make sure parent-teachers get the same service as other parents. If your program provides home visits, staff parents are entitled to them too.

When Nothing Seems to Work

If you give up on working with a family, doing so may feel like a failure to you. Before you give up on establishing a relationship with a family, make sure there are good reasons beyond your own level of frustration. You may have reasons such as these:

- The relationship with the parent will only improve if you take steps that are unethical or illegal.
- The parent's lack of trust is negatively affecting his child's school experience.
- The parent's lack of trust is negatively affecting relationships with other families in the program.
- The parent makes staff members feel unsafe.

A parent who is uncomfortable with the ethnicity, gender, sexual preference, or age of a teacher needs to be educated on the benefits of diversity in the life of her child. By helping a parent work through such issues, you can have a profound effect on the child's life. Take time to help families work through knee-jerk responses to prejudices they might not have even been aware of. For instance, the benefits of having a positive male presence usually outweigh the possible negative fallout. You cannot break the law governing discriminatory hiring practices even if you know parents might be uncomfortable. Once parents develop trust, they will see the unique relationship their child can develop with a male caregiver. This is especially important for children who do not have many men in their lives.

If parents refuse to take part in working with their children's challenging behavior, the program administrator will have to decide if the child can be accommodated without change. This requires a delicate balance of the needs of the individual child, other children in the program, and the staff. NAEYC's "Code of Ethical Conduct" provides assistance in working through when it is appropriate to disenroll a family from your program. Here are some questions that may help you make a decision:

Is the child disruptive? If so, is he disruptive enough to make it difficult for the group to function? Are there changes that can be made to the program (schedule, staffing, or expectations) that will alleviate the disruption?

Is the child thriving in the program? If not, are there changes that can be made (personal attention, new classroom) that will help the child to thrive and grow even if it is not as much as she might with professional intervention?

Is the program's relationship with the family still sound enough to benefit the child? Can parents and staff work together to meet the child's needs, or are too many bad feelings in the way? If it feels too hard, consider whether there are some ways you can change your behavior or your feelings to make the situation better.

If a parent is spreading his negative attitude to other parents and is not responding to attempts from staff to improve the relationship, the family may need to be asked to leave the program.

Staff members need to feel physically and psychologically safe at work. When lack of trust turns to hostility, a teacher is at risk of accusations and may not feel safe in the workplace. For example, when I was a center director, I had a very volatile parent who accused her son's teacher of not liking her child as much as other children and told the teacher she would be "watching her like a hawk" for examples of her son not being treated fairly. I told the parent that we had to meet with the teacher to discuss her concerns before the child could return to school.

If you cannot establish a baseline of trust with a family that allows you to be effective with their child, you may have to help the family leave the program. Be candid with them about your feelings to find out if the placement should continue. You might say, "We seem to be struggling to work together for your child. Perhaps you would be better served with a teacher with whom you can more easily build rapport."

If it is not in the best interest of the child, family, or program to continue the child's enrollment, then make a transition plan with the family to minimize disruption for the child. Give the family ample opportunity to find another placement for their child, refer them to other programs, prepare the child and other children in the program for the change, and assist the family in enrolling in another program by providing records. Other issues that might result in disenrolling children from your program could include the Individuals with Disabilities Education Act (IDEA). Even private programs must meet the requirements of IDEA. There are strict rules governing providing services for children with disabilities.

State licensing rules can also have an impact on enrollment in your program. Check with your state to learn if there are rules that guide your actions.

SCENARIO 1

"What Is Going On at School?," or Building Trust

One teacher complains:

"I have a parent who doesn't seem to believe anything I tell him. It's like he is trying to catch me in a lie. He asks about how his son's day went. When I share information, he looks skeptical and grills me for more information. The other day he asked if his son could come in on his day off. I explained that we have too many children on that day and we can't take another. I saw him going over the sign-in sheets and counting the children! Once his child came home with a cut on his elbow, and the dad asked me how he did it. I explained that he fell on the sidewalk. Not five minutes later, he was asking my teaching assistant what happened! How am I supposed to develop a relationship with a parent who doesn't trust me?"

Dad sees the problem differently:

"It's important to me that I am a responsible parent. My son is too young to always tell me what happens, so I need to check to be sure everything is on the up-and-up. Sometimes I think the school tries to take advantage of ignorant parents—making up rules to suit them. I am just making sure I understand the rules. The teacher is so defensive. It makes me wonder what she has to hide."

WHAT IS THE PROBLEM?

Developing trust is often the first challenge to a relationship between a parent and teacher. Trusting others to care for your child can be scary. The younger the child, the more vulnerable she is, as the child cannot speak for herself. Expecting trust may seem reasonable—who would place their child in a program with people they don't trust? But trust comes in increments. The most basic trust, which needs to happen before parents can leave their children in your care, is trust that their children will not be abused or stolen. Deeper levels of trust—that caregivers will care about and for the child, like and perhaps love the child, understand the child enough to meet her needs, interact with the child as they would at home, and not place the needs of other children before the needs of their child—develop more slowly. If a teacher or parent perceives a lack of trust, problems will arise in relationship building.

Once a climate of distrust has developed, you need to figure out if it can be repaired. Sit down with the family. You may want another person with you to help you communicate. Share what you have experienced with the family and your concern for how it may affect their child. Remember, it is not the family's job to care about you.

WHAT ARE YOU THINKING?

Be aware of how your reaction might make the situation worse. Moving toward positive solutions is easier if you can recognize and avoid certain defensive mindsets that can make it difficult to develop a healthy partnership with parents. Typical defensive reactions include the following:

"The parent doesn't think I am trustworthy." It is hard to keep from personalizing suspicions from parents. Rather, give parents the benefit of the doubt and stay as open as possible. Defensiveness can confirm the parent's feeling of suspicion.

"The parents will undermine my relationship with the child." Children are likely to pick up safety cues from parents. Telling parents to stop acting distrustful in front of their children is not likely to help. Children pick up on the feelings of their parents. When parents' words, feelings, and actions do not match, children become confused.

"The parents will ruin my reputation with other parents." You cannot control relationships among parents. Parents will share concerns with other parents, and all you can do is hope that your relationship with most parents is strong enough for them to ignore the concerns of others.

"This parent is looking for an excuse to remove his child from my school (or class or home)." Sometimes parents need a face-saving reason for removing a child from a program when embarrassing factors prompt a change. It is much easier to tell friends that the program or teacher wasn't good enough than it is to say you can't afford the program or you need longer hours than the program provides. You can make it easier for parents to remove their child from the program by being gracious about the exit so they don't need to find evidence against you.

WHAT ARE PARENTS THINKING?

Thinking about how our actions strike emotional chords with parents (just as their actions have an impact on us) can help us to be more sensitive.

"Here we go again." Parents who have experienced a profound lack of fairness in their own lives, especially in families that are not from the dominant culture, are often eager to protect their children from that experience. If parents are suspicious of you, they may have been lied to in similar situations in the past. It is important to give the message that you will treat all families fairly. This is not about you; it's about society. For some families, you will need to be overt about fairness rather than thinking it will be assumed. Tell families how you have ensured fairness when an action or policy implies fairness but could be viewed as favoring some children (such as enrollment or placement in programs, variable tuition rates, or discipline policies).

"This teacher only shares information with my wife, as if she's the real parent and I am not." Trust can be difficult for both dads and moms for different reasons. Most men are going to feel in the minority in a preschool environment, and most are unaccustomed to that feeling. Separated parents may be especially sensitive. Noncustodial parents can feel out of the loop or that the school takes the side of the custodial parent (often the mother). Mothers can feel powerless to advocate for themselves or their children. If you think a parent is having a difficult time expressing her needs or those of her children, take the time to clarify.

SOLVING THE PROBLEM

Each situation will require unique solutions, but the following are some paths you might take.

Ask parents if they are getting the information they need from you. Say something like, "I am wondering if I am keeping you informed enough about class events. Is a short talk at pickup time working for you?"

Listen to the parents' comments without defensiveness. If you allow them to talk without being interrupted, parents may get past negative feelings and figure out what they really want. They may realize you are not the person they are struggling with. They may share things you have said or nonverbal communication messages they have picked up from you that you are unaware of. For example, when your eyes dart from the parent to a child, the parent may read that move as lack of interest rather than you hyper-vigilantly keeping an eye on the class.

Share your desire for communication. Say something such as, "I wish I had time to talk to you at pickup as well. It seems like as soon as you walk in the door, something comes up that takes my attention."

Ask for suggestions. See what the parent thinks would help to improve information sharing, and create a plan that everyone can live with. "Would phone calls or notes work better?"

AFTER THE PROBLEM IS SOLVED: MOVING TOWARD TRUE PARTNERSHIP

Building trust takes time, and if you stick with the family during the process, it can be very rewarding. In one program, some of the families that teachers struggled with the most eventually established such a strong foundation of trust that they continued to seek our counsel when their child entered high school. The other benefit of building trust is that often families have several children go through the program. You can enjoy a foundation of trust from the beginning when you've already worked with a child's siblings.

Offer families regular opportunities to fill out anonymous questionnaires to give feedback, assess the program, and review your performance. Being able to put their concerns on the table might help them let go. You are likely to receive feedback that can improve your program. Doing this also gives you feedback from many satisfied families. Include information in newsletters or other parent communication about changes you have made in response to questionnaires.

BEFORE YOU HAVE A PROBLEM

The following suggestions can be used to avoid trust problems.

Begin by building a relationship. Acknowledge the need to build trust. When you first meet a family, acknowledge that trust takes time. This can help parents relax

SCENARIO 1

and understand that their feelings are natural. If they feel it is abnormal to have trust issues with a new caregiver, they may be looking for an explanation of what triggered their reaction.

Be available. If you stretch your availability during the early stages of building the relationship, it will be easier for parents to trust that you will find time for them later.

Fear of Men, Strangers, and Dangerous Persons, or The Boogeyman

One teacher shares her dilemma:

"We had our parent open house at the beginning of the year. Mrs. Johnson asked me about the student interns, so I told her about Joe. She became pale. "A man? I don't feel comfortable with that. Maybe I can get my daughter switched into the other class."

Mrs. Johnson explains:

"You read so much about child molesters. I know that they are usually men. It seems like pedophiles get jobs where they have access to children. I would never forgive myself if something happened to my daughter. It just doesn't seem worth taking the chance."

WHAT IS THE PROBLEM?

Emotionally, leaving your child with others is risky enough. Asking parents to accept placing their children in the care of someone they find suspect is even tougher.

Consciousness is heightened in new situations. Just as you begin noticing red Volkswagens once you buy one, placing their child in care makes parents notice any new media story about children in child care. Parents read molestation stories. They know that they are ultimately responsible for what happens to their children. They may be receiving comments and even pressure from relatives. A generation ago, it was less common for men to be involved in the care of children, and to some people, it still seems unnatural.

WHAT ARE YOU THINKING?

Be aware of how your reaction might make the situation worse. Moving toward positive solutions is easier if you can recognize and avoid certain defensive mind-sets that make it difficult to develop a healthy partnership with parents. Typical defensive reactions include the following:

"The parent doesn't trust my judgment." We like to believe that the families we work with trust our decisions unconditionally, but it's appropriate for parents to scrutinize decisions that affect their children. That's their job!

"Parents are interfering with staffing decisions." Parents want and need to know who is caring for their children. You would not approve if parents left their children with a babysitter they didn't know. They also need to know who is taking care of their children in provider-based care.

"The parent is going to make unfair accusations." Unfounded charges of abuse have been a major concern of caregivers for over a decade. The best way to avoid accusations is to keep the parents as informed and involved as possible. If parents feel free to take advantage of an open-door policy, they can learn they have nothing to fear.

WHAT ARE PARENTS THINKING?

Thinking about how our actions strike emotional chords with parents (just as their actions have an impact on us) can help us to be more sensitive.

"Why would a man want to work with young children?" Some people are less comfortable than others with men caring for children. Is the concerned parent ethnically different from the male caregiver? Is she a single mother who may have less experience leaving her child in the care of a male? Is there a religious issue? Knowing the answers to these questions will not necessarily change your policies but may give you insight into how best to approach the family.

SOLVING THE PROBLEM

If a parent has questioned the appropriateness of a male staff member, you may find it hard to keep from becoming defensive. But you can help by providing reassurances.

Explain why you have selected this person to join your staff. Share what you like about him, the special qualifications he has (including his personality), and the extent of your references check.

Share the benefits of having men as caregivers. Some parents will not have considered that nurturing men can enrich their children's lives.

Share positive stories from your experiences. Sharing specific stories about how educators who are men have had a positive affect on the lives of children can be helpful.

Explain the precautions you will take to protect all children and staff. Protecting the men on staff from suspicion is vital. Will they (or any other staff members) be alone with children when toileting or dressing? These activities place men at risk for accusations, and having men take these responsibilities may not be worth the potential problems if there are female staff who can handle these tasks. If a man is teaching alone, will other teachers or parents drop into the classroom unannounced? This may give parents confidence.

AFTER THE PROBLEM IS SOLVED: MOVING TOWARD TRUE PARTNERSHIP

Can you include parent representatives in the hiring process? When parents have personal investment in a staff member's success, they share their enthusiasm with other families. You might even ask a parent who was on the hiring committee to write a welcome letter for the new teacher to share with other families.

BEFORE YOU HAVE A PROBLEM

The following suggestions can be used to avoid problems in trusting new staff members.

Begin by building a relationship. Introduce parents to all staff. Provide introductions in person or through written notices. Have photos and short biographies posted or in promotional materials. Include background information about each staff member. Knowing that a male teacher is someone's son, father, uncle, friend, and so on makes him seem safer. The best way to avoid demonizing a person is by getting to know him or her.

Be trustworthy. Don't make statements that are not true. If all teachers help children in the bathroom or rub backs at naptime, don't pretend that this won't happen.

The Parent Who Drains You, or "Excuse me, but I have some children here who need my attention."

This teacher is overwhelmed by the needs of parents:

"Sarah's mom is so needy. She is single and has no family in this area. I know she's had some health problems as well. But she acts like our job is to take care of her instead of taking care of Sarah. She comes in when we are in the middle of group time, and she always has ten things she has to tell us, like who is picking up Sarah, phone numbers for where we can reach her, some new worry she has from reading her magazines. It's the same routine when she picks up. My teaching partner and I both just want to hide when she comes. She volunteers to help in the classroom on Wednesdays, but then she wants to spend the whole time talking to me instead of working with the children. No offense, but I don't need another girlfriend!"

Sarah's mom explains:

"It is so hard taking care of Sarah by myself. Her father is such a flake—he makes all kinds of promises, but he always lets us down. Sarah is my whole life. I spend a lot of time at her school so I can be the best mother possible. But sometimes it seems like the teachers just don't want to know about Sarah's time at home. They don't seem very friendly when I come into the classroom. It makes me wonder if everything is okay. I mean, don't they want parents to be involved?"

WHAT IS THE PROBLEM?

If a parent has already established a habit of demanding your attention, you need to gently wean her off it. If you withdraw too suddenly, the parent may think she has done something wrong and may put more energy into reconciling. It can be helpful to find a replacement: "Talk to Betsy's mom about that—she mentioned that too."

WHAT ARE YOU THINKING?

Be aware of how your reaction might make the situation worse. Moving toward positive solutions is easier if you can recognize and avoid certain defensive mindsets that can make it difficult to develop a healthy partnership with parents. Typical defensive reactions include these:

"This parent is taking over my classroom." Parents don't always realize that we keep a constant vigil on our classrooms. It appears that we spend some time just standing around. Parents don't think they are distracting us from observing the children.

"This parent expects me to socialize with her, and it interferes with my private life." As difficult as it may be, it's kinder to refuse invitations for social time if you don't want to attend.

WHAT ARE PARENTS THINKING?

Thinking about how our actions strike emotional chords with parents (just as their actions have an impact on us) can help us to be more sensitive.

"She loves my daughter so much, we have a strong connection. We could be friends." Some parents are more isolated and so are needier than others. This can be true of parents who have moved from a different country or who are single parents. While you should not socialize more than you are comfortable doing, you also shouldn't worry that you need to have the same relationship with all parents.

SOLVING THE PROBLEM

Hiding from a needy parent may seem hard to resist, but hiding will not help solve the problem. Taking actions such as those described below can help.

Acknowledge the parent's need for contact. Say something such as, "I can tell you really appreciate the time you spend in our classroom."

Let the parent know that the children are your first priority. Say something such as, "I'm sorry that at times it seems like I am ignoring you, but the children need my constant attention."

Suggest other modes of communication. Say something such as, "Since I can't stop to give you directions when you come in to do a project with the children, how about if I leave written instructions for you on the clipboard?"

Avoid sending double messages. If you say, "Maybe we can meet for coffee sometime," and then you avoid making a firm date, the parent is left confused. Instead, you can say, "When I am not at work, my family (or studies or personal life) requires all of my energy. I'm sorry I won't have time for social engagements with school families."

Try to help the parent connect with others. You can suggest that she join a parenting club if there is one in your area, or you can mention a fellow parent who lives in the area whom she might be able to socialize with.

AFTER THE PROBLEM IS SOLVED: MOVING TOWARD TRUE PARTNERSHIP

Why not include social support for parents as part of your job? If you know that a parent is especially needy, arrange with your coworkers to cover for you so you have time to chat with the parent. It may be a greater service for the child than you can perform in the classroom.

BEFORE YOU HAVE A PROBLEM

The following suggestions can be used to avoid problems with needy parents.

Begin by building a relationship. Set clear limits from the beginning. Teachers are some parents' only regular contact with adults. Parents develop trust in us and appreciate that we love their children. Sometimes they infringe on our boundaries and want us to become a part of their social circle. We may be the only people who give them attention, and they come to depend on it. Establishing limits without hurting their feelings is tricky. Setting boundaries at the beginning is easier and less likely to leave a parent feeling deserted.

Focus on the parents' perspective. Help isolated parents connect with other parents. Offer social events for families and steer parents toward conversation with each other. Caring for parents' social needs is a natural part of a family-friendly program. Perhaps a volunteer parent can arrange family social events. Some schools have group camping trips, family outings on weekends, and other activities to support parents.

Discussion Questions

1. What kind of relationship did your parents have with the programs you attended as a child? How do you think that affected you as a child? What might have strengthened your parents' relationship with your school?

2. Make a list of the parents you get along with the most easily. What do they have in common? Make a list of the parents you have more troubling relationships with. See if you can find similarities that do not blame or judge these families. What steps can you take to move more families from list two to list one?

3. What steps do you take to make parents feel comfortable in your classroom? What else can you try?

CHAPTER 2

Communicating with Families

Communication is one of the most important and challenging parts of working with families. We all have different styles of communication. Often when we are busy working with children, we find it hard to resist blaming parents when communication doesn't go well.

Communication also has a cultural component, and if we are culturally different from the families we serve, this can add another challenge. Some cultures value direct communication. Others find this type of communication aggressive and value a less direct communication style. Some expect eye contact; others find it disrespectful. Some value self-promotion; others expect humble comments about one's self.

Tips for Communicating with Parents

Remember those teachers we mentioned in the introduction? You know, the teachers whom parents always want for their child? The ones parents always want to talk to? The ones who can even give parents criticism that parents will listen to? You can move toward being one of these teachers by building relationships through communication. You can take a number of steps to improve your communication with families:

1. Let parents lead the conversation.
2. Be proactive with information.
3. Focus on parents' perspectives.
4. Plan for addressing problems with parents.

5. Take time to respond thoughtfully to parents' comments and requests.
6. Use the principles of active listening and respectful communication.
7. Give parents the benefit of the doubt.

Let Parents Lead the Conversation

Don't try to direct every conversation. Sometimes the parents who want to share important information will need to get around to the topic in their own way. Mary describes a conversation with a parent:

> *"Johanna was making small talk, but her demeanor didn't match her words. Finally she said, 'We lost the baby last night.' She hadn't told me she was pregnant, but her son had told me. I didn't pretend I didn't know. I didn't make assumptions about how she felt. I just let her tell me in her own way. What she really wanted to know was how to tell her son Luke."*

Be Proactive with Information

Emily's mom said the following:

> *"It was amazing! I drove up to pick up my child from school, and there was an ambulance in the driveway. I ran up to the door, terrified that something had happened to Emily. There was the teacher, greeting us with information before we entered the classroom: 'The children are listening to a story with Sally (the other teacher). One of the children in our class had a seizure at school. We had to call an ambulance to care for her.' She then handed us a preprinted letter that addressed how to talk to our children about seizures, which they had written in case something like this happened. Because I was informed, I was able to calm Emily rather than having her deal with a scared mommy."*

Sometimes we avoid telling parents about less pleasant experiences in the hope they won't find out, thinking that what they don't know won't hurt them. The information may be for the whole parent body (a lice outbreak or a teacher leaving the program) or for a specific family (a child getting hurt at school or losing a belonging that is later found). Holding back information is a bad policy for two reasons. First, parents will not trust us if they learn we are keeping secrets. They will feel it is necessary to dig up information that is being hidden from them. As they investigate, we become less forthcoming, and the relationship dissolves. Second, it is damaging for children to have experiences their parents cannot help them understand. Even if parents never find out something you didn't want them to know, it is harder for children to deal with uncomfortable memories they are harboring if their parents do not know or understand their experience. Parents can accept almost anything if they are told honestly and assured that mistakes won't happen again. I have known of parents forgiving teachers for forgetting children on field trips, accidentally hurting a child, saying something careless, and even losing control of their temper.

Share daily experiences with parents often enough that they are not startled by a request for communication. If parents are not accustomed to chatting with you or receiving written communication, contact will take on greater importance. Slipping something into conversation is easier when communication happens often.

Focus on the Parent's Perspective

Give parents information as it pertains to their child, their roles as parents, and how it affects their lives. They are less likely to be concerned with the needs of the whole class, your needs, or the school's needs than they are with their own needs and the needs of their children. This is not a matter of being selfish. The parents' job is to think about the needs of their child and family. Your job is to balance the needs of all of the children and the program as a whole and to find a solution that works for everyone.

This parent believes her request is reasonable:

> *"I just asked if my daughter could stay awake during naptime. We are flying out tonight to visit my folks, and I wanted her to sleep on the plane. The teacher started telling me that she makes all her phone calls while the kids are sleeping and how it would be hard for her to keep my daughter awake. She's not the one who has to be on that plane with a restless child who won't sleep!"*

Focusing on the parent's perspective means not expecting the parent to care about your needs and issues. If you respond with "But I need the children all to sleep because that is when I get my paperwork done," you are expecting the parent to place your paperwork over the needs of her child. Another answer parents will not appreciate is, "If I let you do it, then I will have to let other parents do it." A reasonable response for parents would be to explain what research shows about overly tired children fussing more and having a harder time sleeping. Another response might be just letting the child stay awake.

To keep yourself focused on the parent's perspective so you can solve the problem, ask yourself questions like these:

How does this issue directly affect the parent? Focus on the outcomes for the parent. The impact on the class, the other children, the other families, or the teacher is not the parents' problem and does not directly affect them.

What do you want the parent to do? Be clear in your message. Are you asking for parental action? You may just want to let parents know that their child had a meltdown before lunch, but you don't expect them to do anything. If this meltdown is a continuing problem, you may ask the parents to take action. If you do want action, have a couple of alternatives in mind. Maybe you could suggest that the child eat breakfast before school or that the parents let you know if he doesn't eat so you can offer an earlier snack.

Are you keeping an open mind? If you are unwilling to accept any alternative solution, you are likely to experience conflict.

Are you truly listening to the parent's point of view? If you are thinking about how you are going to respond to what the parent is saying or prove her wrong, you are not truly listening.

If you start communicating with an understanding of the parents' perspective, you can choose your words more carefully and use language that is more relevant and meaningful to them. Communicating with parents is not the same as communicating with colleagues. One thing to consider is that the language we use may be meaningless to parents. However, there are ways we can teach parents the vocabulary of education they may have heard over the years without making them feel ignorant.

Avoid using technical jargon. You can introduce teacherese with an explanation to prepare parents for future teacher interactions. Changing teacher jargon to parent-friendly language can look like this:

Instead of saying	*Use parent-friendly language*	*Follow up with an example*
Manipulatives	Toys that children put together by hand	"Sally used Legos to build a house. That shows she can use her body to create what her mind thought up. We call toys like Legos *manipulatives*."
Cognitive development	Developing thinking	"I saw that Johnny is developing his thinking skills when he thought of using the funnel to fill the bottle with water. We call developing thinking *cognitive development*."
Developmentally appropriate practice (DAP)	Making sure that we are providing activities and have expectations that match what we know about young children	"We encourage Maggie to write her name even if she gets some of the letters wrong. At her age, she is still learning about writing. We say that offering these activities that challenge children but aren't too hard are *developmentally appropriate*."
Sociodramatic play	Pretending	"It is great to see Sammy starting to pretend to call Mama on the toy telephone. It is a sign that he is remembering what he has seen and is working to understand it. We call that *sociodramatic play*."
Fine-motor and gross-motor development	Body development	"Hunter is walking up the steps now on the slide. We call developing the use of his body *gross-motor development*."
Social and emotional development	Developing understanding of feelings	"Yesterday Molly said she felt frustrated. She is learning to identify her feelings. We call that *emotional development*."

Instead of saying	***Use parent-friendly language***	***Follow up with an example***
Self-regulation	Self-control	"Tommy was really mad, but he didn't hit the other child. He told the child that he was mad. He is learning to control his feelings and body. We call that *self-regulation*."
Environmental print	Written words around us	"Gabriella looked at the exit sign above the door and said, 'That means go out.' That shows that she is paying attention to words around her. We call that *environmental print*."
Book-handling skills	Learning about reading	"Jonas was turning pages in *Brown Bear* and saying the words he remembered. He is showing us that he is learning about how reading works. We call that *book-handling skills*."

Plan for Addressing Problems with Parents

We all have times when we need to tell parents about a problem. Keep the following in mind when you communicate with families about problems.

Practice with a Colleague If You Are Not Sure What to Say and How to Say It

This teacher describes her problem:

> *"Boy, did I step in it. I just tried to mention to Mrs. Jones, as she was picking up Doug, that he pocketed a toy car today. Could she check to be sure he didn't have any other school toys at home? She just blew up! Said her child wasn't a thief! Made a scene in front of the other parents!"*

If you are a novice teacher, have particularly difficult information to share with a parent, or have not developed a positive relationship with the parent, you may benefit from practicing the conversation with a colleague. If the colleague will take the role of devil's advocate or that of a difficult parent, you can be better prepared for the conversation.

Some questions to discuss together include the following:

1. **What is the best timing for the topic?** Sometimes it is important to talk to parents right away (before they hear about it from someone else, such as their child). At other times, it is better to let everyone cool down before broaching the topic.
2. **How will you bring up the topic?** Talk through your opener. Should you be prepared with resources? If you are talking to a parent about a concern that involves his or her child, it will help if you can provide supporting articles, brochures, or community resource information.
3. **Should you invite a colleague to join in the discussion?** If tempers are likely to flare or you are concerned about being misquoted, having a coteacher or director with you might help. If nothing else, you might want to make sure someone else is in the building.
4. **How can you share information as clearly as possible without being too blunt?** It can be hard to hear what you are saying from the perspective of the listener, especially if it is a difficult message. You may find that role-playing the conversation with a coworker can help.

Keep a Calm Demeanor Even If You Are Nervous

It is easy for parents to pick up on our anxiety.

This teacher describes how her nervousness made a situation worse:

> *"I had to tell Jonah's parents that he used a bad word at school. I know they are really devoutly religious, and I didn't know how they were going to react. Were they going to think we talk that way at school? When they came to pick him up, I asked them to come into the hallway to talk to me, and I let Jonah play in the classroom with my teaching assistant. They looked really concerned and asked me what was wrong. I explained that Jonah had used a bad word at school. They asked what word, and I told them. They laughed and said that he heard an older kid at the ball field say that and he had been repeating it. They were just ignoring it so he wouldn't think he could get attention for using it. His dad said, 'You were so serious, we were afraid something was really wrong! You've got to lighten up!' Boy, was he right!"*

The following are some suggestions for keeping calm:

1. Use calming body language. Parents pick up on nonverbal cues.
2. Balance your weight firmly over your feet so you are grounded.
3. Smile and make eye contact, facing the parents directly unless this is culturally inappropriate.
4. Don't forget to breathe!

Begin with Assurances That Everything Is Okay

Sometimes people don't listen when they are waiting for the punch line. If you start by giving a lot of context, describing what happened first, or start with excuses, parents are going to get more and more anxious. To prevent that, a conversation about a child getting hurt can start: "She's okay now, but . . . ," or a conversation about a child's misbehavior can start: "She understands now, but . . ."

Gauge If the Situation Needs Privacy for the Discussion

Deanna describes when her comments created an unpleasant scene:

> *"Penny's mom sent a cupcake in her lunch box. We don't allow children to bring sweets to school except for special occasions. I noticed the cupcake and slipped it out of Penny's lunch box before lunchtime, and she never noticed. I was telling Penny's mom about it when she picked her up, and she turned red and started yelling at me. Penny overheard and started crying for her cupcake. After they left, Samantha's mom asked me what that was all about. I didn't want to tell her because I didn't think I should tell her that Penny's mom broke the school rule."*

The following are some considerations about when to make a conversation private:

- If you are unsure about the parent's reaction, don't bring it up in front of the child. If the child reacts to the tension between you and the parent, the whole situation can escalate. In this case, find a private place to have a conversation with the parent.
- Talk to the parent out of earshot of other parents. In a confidential conversation, one of the worst things that can happen is for

another parent to hear part of the interaction. Because of confidentiality, you would be unable to tell other parents anything about the conversation with the first parent. Thus, the parent who overheard could end up having to make up a story in her own mind to explain what she overheard. For example, a parent might overhear part of a conversation about a toy getting lost and assume that the teacher and parent were talking about a child getting lost.

Make Arrangements for Follow-Up Conversation If Necessary

It may be that you have told parents something they need to digest before the dialogue continues. Suggest that they call you later or agree to meet them at school early the next day. In other situations, parents may agree to a solution to a problem on the spot, but when they get home and talk to other family members about it, they may change their minds. If you have invited them to think about it and talk more later, no one loses face by having to go back on an agreement.

Avoid Giving Unwelcome News in Writing before Verbal Contact

This is especially a problem with e-mail. If information needs to go in writing, it should follow a conversation. Don't forget that anything you put in writing can be read by others (including lawyers!) without the supporting context.

Take Time to Respond Thoughtfully to Parents' Comments and Requests

Kiko is a new teacher:

> *"Timmy's mom asked me if I thought he was ready for kindergarten. I said, 'Sure.' I mentioned the conversation with the head teacher, and she disagreed. She thinks he's too immature. I don't know how to bring it up to the mom now."*

If a parent brings an issue to you, don't be afraid to tell her you need to think about what she has said or gather more information. Here are some steps to keep you out of trouble:

Take time to cool down if the conversation is heated or pushes your buttons. You can't take back words once they are said.

Make sure you have the authority to make promises if asked. Giving permission to parents to do something out of the ordinary, and later telling them your supervisor doesn't approve, makes both you and your supervisor look bad.

Take the time you need to gather information. One school superintendent vowed to always return calls from parents within twenty-four hours, which sometimes proved to be a bad idea. She didn't always take time to gather facts first. By taking the time to respond most appropriately, you demonstrate to parents that you are taking their issue seriously.

If there is a delay in getting back to the parents, let them know you haven't forgotten. If you are waiting for information, let parents know what the holdup is (for example, you're waiting to speak to the director, who is on vacation, or you want to check licensing regulations) and when you will respond. You don't want to give the impression you are ignoring the conversation in hopes that parents will forget about it.

Use the Principles of Active Listening and Respectful Communication

Rita shares how she uses experience from her personal life to improve her communication with parents:

> *"My husband and I are in counseling, and I find the same advice our counselor gives us about how to communicate also works well with the parents. I had a mom come to me, ready to really let me have it. She was mad because her daughter's stuffed animal was lost. I pulled her aside, listened to her without interrupting, and demonstrated that I understood her by saying, 'This isn't the first time Boo-Boo has been lost. It's really frustrating, and I know Sierra can't sleep without Boo-Boo.' Then I made a commitment for a short-term and a long-term solution: 'Let's find Boo-Boo now, and tonight I'll think about how we can keep this from happening again.' We looked around and found the bear, and the mom relaxed. She suggested buying another bear like Boo-Boo so it wouldn't be a problem if the bear was lost again. It was great that she went from being mad at me to feeling like we are a team."*

Communication between parents and early childhood educators should reflect the best of what we know about respectful communication. We have ongoing relationships with parents, and strained communication won't help. Children notice the relationship between the important people in their lives—their parents and their teachers—and any tension will upset them. It is especially rewarding when you see the respectful communication techniques you are using find their way into the communication between parents and their children. Here are some cues for respectful communication:

Listen attentively. Don't interrupt. Hear the feelings that drive the words.

Demonstrate that you understand the message of the parent. Phrases such as "I hear you saying . . ." or "It sounds like . . ." may feel stilted when you try to use them, so find a way of expressing these ideas that fits you. Some teachers use "I wonder if . . ." or "Do you feel . . ." as other ways to reflect back.

Use words to express that you understand the issue from their perspective. If parents don't think you get it, they may give up or become frustrated. When you show that you understand why they feel the way they do, parents may be ready to move to finding a solution. It also gives you the opportunity to correct your assumptions if you have read the situation wrong. You might think a parent is angry when she is actually worried. If you don't understand, ask.

Be sure to avoid blaming the parent for the situation. If you are raising a difficult issue, describe the problem in nonjudgmental terms, the consequences of the problem, and, if appropriate, your feelings. It may be that your feelings need to be kept out of the situation to keep the interaction professional. For example, "When you are late picking up Abby, I am late picking up my daughter at her school, and she worries if I'm late" gives clear cause-and-effect information. "When you are late picking up Abby, you are making me the bad mother picking up my daughter late" is less professional.

Keep the conversation on track. If the parent becomes accusatory, don't take the bait. You can say, "I'm sorry you feel that way, but right now we need to find a solution for this issue that will work for all of us." If the parent brings up unrelated issues to put you on the defense, you can say, "Let's talk about that when we are done dealing with this issue." Be specific rather than general about the situation you're trying to solve.

Avoid inflammatory words. Generalizing about peoples' behavior makes them feel judged and defensive. Describe the events that need to be talked about (for example, "You have picked up Abby ten minutes late twice this week, and tonight you are thirty minutes late") rather than generalizing about the behavior (for example, "You are irresponsible about pickup time"). Words to avoid include *rude, disrespectful, selfish,* or other words you would not want people to use to describe you.

When you've found a solution, say it again. Restating is a way of clarifying and making sure that you have understood each other. Try saying something such as, "So you are going to write his name on his shoes. I will check after nap to see that they are in his cubby." The parent has a chance to hear the expectation and can correct it if necessary.

Give Parents the Benefit of the Doubt

Sharon shares what she learned:

> *"I used to get so annoyed with Felice's mother. I would give her information about school procedures. She'd nod and say, 'Okay,' but she would never follow through. I finally realized she doesn't understand English as well as I thought she did. Now I take more time to show her what I mean, and I can see in her eyes if she understands me."*

Lilian Katz, noted expert on both early childhood and teacher education, believes all of us have a tendency at times to attribute our own mistakes to circumstances (traffic was bad, clocks were wrong) but to assign other people's mistakes to character flaws ("She's flaky." "She comes late because she likes to make an entrance.") (Katz 1995). Assuming people have positive intentions changes this tendency and concentrates our attention on the circumstances at hand. Positive expectations and a strong sense of forgiveness count for much when it comes to communicating.

When Nothing Seems to Work

What are signs that communication is so compromised that a child and parents are not benefiting from the program? It is tempting to give up on families quickly, but your program may be the first school experience for many families. Taking the time to build positive communication can influence their child's whole school career.

Asking families to leave should always be a last resort. One reason it might be necessary is when communication with families is so compromised that the child is suffering. Some examples include:

- Children are consistently told to keep secrets from their teachers and have severe reactions when asked for information. This may be about illness, living arrangements, or exposure to unhealthy experiences.
- Parents misquote the teacher consistently in a destructive manner. This may come up with divorced families, other parents, or the community outside of the school.
- Lack of communication is having a detrimental effect on the child. This may happen when families don't responding to important requests, aren't available in case of emergency, or refuse to communicate about the child's behavior at school.

Recommending a Child for Assessment, or "What is wrong with Tim?"

One teacher shares:

"I have been working with children for years, and I have good instincts about when something is just a phase a child is going through and when there is a problem. We've been talking to Tim's parents since he started the year. We gave him the benefit of the doubt for the first month of school, but he just wasn't catching on to routines as fast as I expected. We let his parents know what was going on. We'd give them a quick report at pickup time, and they seemed like they appreciated the information. We had our first parent-teacher conferences this week, and we told his parents we wanted to have Tim screened. We had the papers right there and everything so we could get right on it. The educational coordinator of our program was there, too, so she could explain how the process worked. Tim's parents seemed really eager to follow through and signed the papers right away. They asked if we thought they should take him to a child psychologist, and we advised them to wait until we saw the screening results. Well, that was Friday, and they haven't brought Tim to school all week. Wednesday they called the director, really upset, ready to take Tim out of the school. They told her that we don't like Tim! What happened between Friday and Monday?"

Tim's parents explain:

"We put Tim in a new school this year, and we've been really happy until now. The teachers really seemed on top of things. We had confidence that all was well. On Friday we had our first conference and found out that the teachers think something is really wrong with Tim. We had no

warning and just walked into this meeting to find one of the program administrators there with papers to sign to have Tim tested for being autistic or something. We were so shocked, we didn't know what to say. I felt so ashamed that my son was in such trouble and I didn't even know it! They seemed to have it all together—knew who we could take our child to—so we were relieved that there was a plan of action. Once we got home, I called my sister-in-law, who is a psychologist. She said there's nothing wrong with Tim. The behavior the teachers described is perfectly normal, she says. We were relieved that she didn't think there was anything wrong with Tim, but now we realize that the teachers think he is a problem. We don't feel like we should even bring him back there."

WHAT IS THE PROBLEM?

Multiple issues are involved in this case. Most are related to the teachers and parents not understanding each other's perspective. One of parents' greatest fears is that there is something wrong with their child.

Parents are worried about their children's future. One of the important phases in a parent's development is the imagining phase (Galinsky 1987), when parents make pictures in their minds of their children as adults, including their occupations and families. A possible developmental delay can change that image.

Parents may feel guilty. It's hard for parents to think that someone else noticed something about their child that they missed. If parents can't trust doctors and other professionals who have cared for their child to have picked up on these problems, they begin to question what else doctors and others could have missed.

Parents may blame themselves. It's easy for parents to feel responsible if something is wrong with their child. Was it their genes? They may remember relatives who have had problems. Was it bad parenting? Maybe it's from that glass of wine Mom had when she was pregnant or from going back to work too soon or being too permissive.

WHAT ARE YOU THINKING?

Be aware of how your reaction might make the situation worse. Moving toward positive solutions is easier if you can recognize and avoid certain defensive mindsets that can make it difficult to develop a healthy partnership with parents. Typical defensive reactions include these:

"If I don't get this child help, I will be irresponsible." You are aware of the benefits of early intervention. In the past few years, teachers have felt a greater sense of responsibility to take advantage of opportunities for early identification. The bottom line: it is ultimately the parents' responsibility.

"These parents are just in denial." Being patient while parents work through their own feelings is difficult. It is hard for a teacher who has not been a parent to relate to the complexity of emotions a parent might feel who has just been confronted with the possibility of a child's abnormal or delayed development.

"They don't trust my judgment." When confronted with something you don't want to believe, it is natural to look to others to support your position. If you are not gracious about parents' need to get corroboration, you may permanently damage the relationship you have with the parents.

WHAT ARE PARENTS THINKING?

Thinking about how our actions strike emotional chords with parents (just as their actions have an impact on us) can help us to be more sensitive.

"The teacher doesn't understand my child." Behaviors that may seem atypical to you in a child may be more typical of children in her cultural group. Self-help skills (feeding, dressing, toileting) are expected at an early age in mainstream American culture. However, in some cultures, these skills are not expected or taught until much later. Second-language learners may understand less than they appear to. Keep in mind that some children's atypical behavior may be related to how much they understand you when you talk to them.

"The teacher is saying my child is dumb!" Different cultural groups have varied attitudes toward doctors, mental health specialists, and differently abled people. Do your homework to find out about families' attitudes and beliefs before talking to them about your concerns.

SOLVING THE PROBLEM

If you plan to talk to parents about concerns about their child's development, you can take steps to ensure a positive outcome. When approached with sensitivity, parents can team up with you to learn about their child's needs and how to best meet them.

Provide parents information about screening. Learn whether the parents' health insurance provides screening, or pass on the names of public organizations that can provide evaluations. If parents are resistant to recommendations that their child be assessed, you will need to ensure that you have given them clear information, made resources available, and repaired any uneasiness between family and school.

Take a step back. Assure parents that you have their child's best interests at heart, and give them time to think through your suggestions. Be clear in your attitude and in your behavior. The parents are the decision makers where their child is concerned.

Be conscious of your behavior toward both the child and family. The parents may be a little wary or defensive as a result of the interaction. Be sure that you do not react defensively or cautiously. The family needs to know that nothing has changed because of the interaction.

Make a plan with the parents to meet again. Give parents time to think about what you have said, and then plan to discuss the issue again. Arrange another meeting for a time that works for the parents, and invite them to bring along a support person, such as a grandparent or family friend.

Cooperate in screening. Many screening tools include checklists or questionnaires to be completed by the teacher.

Be available for parents' questions or concerns during the process. Parents have a lot of information to absorb and decisions to make. You can help.

Learn what you can about meeting the needs of this child. Identifying a child as having special needs doesn't make that child a lesser member of your class. Often, special educators, speech pathologists, and other therapists recommend doing just the kinds of activities that we typically provide in preschool. Rather than focusing on a diagnosis, find out what you can do to help a child with this specific set of behaviors or gaps in understanding. Share your successes with parents and invite their suggestions and ideas.

AFTER THE PROBLEM IS SOLVED: MOVING TOWARD TRUE PARTNERSHIP

Teachers can be great assets to a team putting together an Individual Educational Plan (IEP) for a child with a disability or delay. Home visits from the teaching staff can add insight. Encourage parents to observe the child in school for additional insights too. If the child needs special services, a teacher can be an important member of the team even if services are provided elsewhere. Speech pathologists, occupational therapists, and other specialists can suggest ideas for classroom routines and activities. Teachers can offer ideas for favorite activities and ways to win the child's cooperation with the specialists. It is a great relief for parents to have the teacher they have learned to trust involved in their child's special education.

BEFORE YOU HAVE A PROBLEM

The following suggestions can be used to avoid problems when children are showing signs of special needs.

Be proactive with information. Invite parents to spend time in the classroom. If parents see how their child behaves compared to other children in her class, they may already have a feeling for what you're going to tell them.

Focus on the parents' perspective. Find out how parents view their child. This can happen in a conference before the child enters the program or in a home visit. Communicate with parents with an open mind. Listen to what they have to say about their child and give their opinions credence. There may be other explanations for the behavior you see.

Take time to react. Record observations of the child so you have clear examples to give parents. Share your observations and thoughts.

SCENARIO

5

When Parents Don't Read Your Newsletters, or "Why didn't you tell me she has a field trip today?"

Jenny is frustrated:

"Emiko's mom never bothers to read my newsletters. I value parents knowing what we are doing in our class, and I work hard on my newsletters. I give updates of what we are doing, provide parenting information, and even include illustrations. Today was the last straw. We were supposed to go to the fire station at 8:00. I had it in the newsletter. We were waiting around for Emiko, and her mother finally brought her at 8:15. She blamed me, saying that she didn't know we had a field trip!"

Emiko's mom sees it differently:

"Miss Jenny really embarrassed me in front of the whole class today. I came in at 8:15 like I always do, and she said, "We were about to leave without Emiko! Did you forget we have a field trip today?" How can I forget what I didn't know? She writes these long newsletters and expects us to memorize the whole thing. I don't have time for that!"

WHAT IS THE PROBLEM?

Jenny is using a method of communicating with parents that clearly doesn't work for Emiko's mom. She takes pride in her newsletters and forgets about her audience.

Parents aren't thinking about how teachers prefer to communicate; they are focused on getting the information they need. Keep in mind that teaching is your job. While parenting is the job of any parent, communicating with their child's school is only a small part of it. For parents who work, are single, and/or have more than one child, getting information in a form that requires the least amount of energy is important.

Many younger parents are more accustomed to electronic communication. If we want parents to get the information we are providing, we will be most successful if we use the communication method that is most familiar.

Parents are busy. Receiving information from their child's teacher is one of many tasks a parent completes each day. Oftentimes, if the communication method is inconvenient or inconsistent, the message can be missed.

WHAT ARE YOU THINKING?

Be aware of how your reaction might make the situation worse. Moving toward positive solutions is easier if you can recognize and avoid certain defensive mindsets that can make it difficult to develop a healthy partnership with parents. Typical defensive reactions include these:

"She doesn't care about all of the hard work I put into newsletters." It isn't a parent's job to care about your efforts. Move away from your own emotions and focus on what you hope to accomplish.

"She doesn't value what we do at school." Reading newsletters isn't evidence of caring about school. It has more to do with a parent's preferred method of getting information.

"She just expects me to make do when she doesn't follow through on what I've told her she needs to do." Don't personalize the experience. Find a way to make it work.

WHAT ARE PARENTS THINKING?

Thinking about how our actions strike emotional chords with parents (just as their actions have an impact on us) can help us to be more sensitive.

"Jenny cares more about her pretty newsletters than giving me the information I need." Ask parents how they want to receive communication.

"I am so embarrassed. The other parents were looking at me." When a parent is put on the spot, it is hard for her to focus on what led to the issue rather than on her strong feelings.

SOLVING THE PROBLEM

Rather than putting the parent on the spot when you are both under stress, welcome the child and get ready to go. Communication in these circumstances won't be productive.

Think about using e-mail to send newsletters. Many parents value the information that takes place in a long newsletter, but a hard copy can be lost. It is also harder for parents who don't live together to have access to the same information.

Provide time-sensitive information in multiple ways. Some programs have a whiteboard near the front door for parents to check when they drop off and pick up. A quick text might also be useful. Or consider sending a simple note with information about important events rather than embedding them in longer newsletters.

Give reasons for expectations. If you just say, "You must arrive at 7:45 for the field trip" the parents may think you are being overly controlling. Giving a short explanation about a bus being ready, the firefighters waiting, and the children struggling to wait will help parents understand your perspective, and they will be more likely to comply.

AFTER THE PROBLEM IS SOLVED: MOVING TOWARD TRUE PARTNERSHIP

Taking action to improve and individualize communication will make your life easier. Parents will also feel they are valuable members of the team if they know you care enough to communicate with them effectively.

Conduct a survey with parents at the beginning of each year to learn about their preferred methods of communication. You can individualize communication for parents, such as e-mailing some and posting notes for others. It may seem like a pain to individualize, but it is better than parents not getting the information they need.

Ask a parent to be in charge of communicating general information. This can be a nice way for parents who cannot help in a classroom to be involved in the life of the program. It is not appropriate to give out confidential information, but information about field trips, volunteer activities, and so forth works well with this method.

BEFORE YOU HAVE A PROBLEM

The following suggestions can be used to avoid problems when you're struggling to communicate information to parents.

Focus on the parent's perspective. Thinking about the communication needs of families before investing a lot of time in newsletters will minimize your frustration and resentment.

Plan for addressing problems with parents. If you have a plan for talking to parents about miscommunication, you can avoid possible power struggles.

Use the principles of active listening and respectful communication. You can find out what is keeping families from following through on communication.

Give parents the benefit of the doubt. Assume that parents are doing their best, care about their children's school experience, and have a good reason for not responding to your communication.

Discussion Questions

1. Think about your own communication style. How does it relate to your own culture? What challenges have you had communicating with people in your personal life? How can you apply that to your communication with families?

2. As you read through this chapter, what ideas can help you in your communication with families? Set at least one goal for using new communication strategies.

3. Do you have a colleague who can help you communicate with parents? Are you willing to approach that colleague to ask for help?

CHAPTER 3

Policies That Work for Families and Staff

Written policies have a strong effect on families' experiences in a program. A clearly written policy gives parents the power of information and can help them to feel less vulnerable to the whims of a teacher or administrator. It can give a teacher the leverage to insist on actions that reflect the program's philosophy. It can ensure consistency from one similar situation to the next.

How policies are set and carried out often demonstrates attitudes about children, families, and staff. Policies can reflect defensive positions that assume families and program staff are adversaries or permissive positions that place the wishes of the few over the needs of others. Or policies can be carefully thought out and applied, designed to serve the range of needs of all the parties involved.

Some attitudes drive policies that do not reflect a climate of partnership.

1. The Lead Foot—when policies start with the assumption that if you give an inch, parents will take a mile. "If we let her do that, we'll have to let everyone." This reflects a lack of understanding that people and situations vary. When parents experience rules without reason, their reaction is typical of all humans—fighting against tyranny by breaking the rules.
2. The Oil Can—the habit of oiling the squeaky wheel, the parent who complains. The rules are ignored with a whisper of "Don't tell anyone else I am letting you do this." The message is that either the rule

wasn't valuable enough to enforce or that all rules are up for grabs. If you aren't ashamed of your actions, why keep them a secret? Rather than garnering loyalty from parents, this behavior encourages them to push harder to get their way. It also places less assertive parents at a disadvantage.

3. The Door Mat—giving in to all demands—the philosophy of "the customer is always right." Early childhood educators tend to be uncomfortable with conflict and sometimes will do anything to avoid it. When administrators take this approach, they place staff in a difficult place of having to advocate for themselves. If teachers don't advocate for themselves and the school's policies in the absence of the director's support, parents are robbed of hearing the teacher's perspective on how the original policies can benefit their children.

So what is the alternative? Developing policies based on the values and goals of the families and staff of the program. If a policy is based on the program's philosophy and goals, it is no longer about power struggles. It's about how the community of the program can best meet the needs of all its members.

Principles of Setting and Following Family-Friendly Policies

Three steps will give you a context for thinking about how to set and carry out policies:

1. Create fair policies that support the mission and goals of the program.
2. Tell parents about policies before enrollment.
3. Develop and tend to your relationships with parents.

Step 1: Create Fair Policies

The first step is to know the laws and rules that affect your program and to create policies that are consistent with these rules. For example, most programs are governed by some form of licensing. Rules about health and safety are affected by licensing standards. The National Association for the Education of Young Children (NAEYC) has a voluntary accreditation system. Setting policies that are in conflict with NAEYC's criteria limits the program's ability to receive accreditation. And even private programs are responsible for adhering to the Americans with Disabilities Act (ADA). Creating policies that exclude children and staff with special needs are likely to be in conflict with this law.

With information about laws and rules in mind, create fair policies that support the mission and goals of the program that do not conflict with rules and laws.

Examples of inconsistency between a program's mission and policies:

- If the program's mission is to provide child care for the children of college students, the policies should be consistent with that mission. An example of inconsistency between the mission and policies might be a policy of closing the program during finals week.
- If a program's mission is to nurture a specific culture, the policies should be consistent with that culture. If that culture highly values extended family, a policy stating that only parents can attend school events might be an inconsistency.

Examples of inconsistency between program goals and policy:

- If a program goal is to meet individual children's needs, a policy that requires children to be toilet trained before moving from the toddler classroom to the preschool classroom might be an inconsistency.
- If a program goal is to collaborate with parents in meeting the needs of their children, a policy that parent-teacher conferences are held only during school hours might be an inconsistency.
- If a program goal is to support family engagement, a policy that severely limits families' opinions regarding curriculum and policies might be an inconsistency.

Write down your policies, and make sure all staff and parents have copies. Many preschool programs enjoy a level of informality that seems inconsistent with written policies. Remember, when the policy is written and consistently followed, employees and parents who join the community have the opportunity to know what they are signing on for.

Write policies clearly. Avoid jargon or legalese. If parents don't understand what you are saying, you can't expect them to comply. The table below gives a few examples of policies that are written in a manner than might be difficult for parents to understand and ways to rewrite them in a more parent-friendly manner.

Types of policies	*An example*	*Reasons for confusing language*	*Ways to make the written policy more parent-friendly*
Policies with legalese regarding discrimination	"______ will not discriminate against any child or parent based on race, color, creed, sex, national origin, handicapping condition, or ancestry."	Some programs are required to use very specific language to meet requirements for federal and other funding. Some of this language is very confusing or unclear—such as "creed" and "handicapping condition."	This required statement can be followed up with examples like: "We do not use children's race, culture, whether they are boys or girls, or whether they have special needs to decide if they can attend our program."
Policies about discipline	"We use developmentally appropriate strategies for handling misbehavior."	This does not really tell parents what you will do, when, and why. It also doesn't provide information about what is considered misbehavior. Is it hitting another child? Talking without raising your hand first?	Providing examples of both what is considered to be misbehavior and what might be done will help parents understand. "We do not allow children to hurt one another, but we understand that they are still learning to relate to others. For example, if a child takes a toy away from another child, we would help her ask the other child for a turn and help her find another toy to use while she waits for her turn."
Policies about accommodations	"______ will make all reasonable modifications to our policies and practices to accommodate children with special needs, unless to do so would be a fundamental alteration of our existing program."	Legally, programs cannot refuse to admit children with special needs except in certain situations. One of the exceptions is when including the child would "fundamentally alter the program." This language may be confusing to a family, and if they don't understand what it means, their confusion is more likely to lead to problems.	Providing examples may assist. For example: "Our nature-based preschool uses care and handling of animals as a fundamental part of our curriculum. Inclusion of a child with allergies to animal dander would require a fundamental change in our program."

Types of policies	*An example*	*Reasons for confusing language*	*Ways to make the written policy more parent-friendly*
Assessment policies	"______ uses the ______ as a formal assessment tool. The purpose of the assessment is to determine if child's development is within the range of normalcy. These assessments are completed on each child through anecdotal notes."	"Formal assessment tool," "normalcy," and "anecdotal notes" can be confusing vocabulary for parents who are not professional educators.	Simpler language can be substituted, such as "We use a program called ______. It directs us to write down what we see each child accomplish at school and compare their development with what is expected of children at this age."

State clearly if you make exceptions to any of your policies (for example, rules about enrolling only toilet-trained children may exempt children with special needs without an exception, or different rules may exist for different ages of children).

Be up front about the consequences parents face if they don't follow policies. For example, what happens if a parent is continually late picking his child up from school? Can he keep coming late as long as he pays the late fee, or are there only a certain number of late pickups before a child is disenrolled? It may seem negative to bring up consequences in the beginning. But people deserve to know what could happen, and it takes the pressure off you if you must follow through. Avoid giving double messages. We tend to want to be nice and say, "That's okay," when it clearly is not.

Step 2: Tell Parents about Policies before Enrollment

The second step is to inform parents about policies before they enroll their child. Merely handing out a parent handbook and expecting parents to read and understand the ramifications of all policies is unreasonable. A parent who visits multiple programs to make a placement is overwhelmed with information. Be sensitive to the culture and first language of parents, which can affect both their understanding of policies and their comfort in bringing up concerns.

Spend time talking about policies when parents tour the school. For example, if you have strict hours of operation, make that clear. Some programs allow parents to sign up for extra hours as needed, and they may assume your program does the same.

Talk to parents when their children are enrolling. Make it safe for parents to share conflicts and concerns about policies. If they sense that you might not accept their child into the program if they question policies, they may not verbalize their feelings. It is better to work through any compromises or special circumstances before the child begins.

Give reasons for policies. Some parents really bristle at hearing, "That's the policy," and need a good reason to follow it, especially if it makes their lives more difficult. For example, it might not be obvious to parents that if your program is *campus-related,* it means that your calendar is linked to the schedule of the college.

Step 3: Develop and Tend to Your Relationships with Parents

The third step is to develop and tend to your relationships with parents. It is important to develop rapport and a sense of trust with families before conflicts come up. If you have established a good, trusting relationship with parents, it will be easier to get them to comply with policies they don't agree with, especially when they understand that doing so is important to you.

Be flexible and compromise whenever possible. Keep your eye on the reason for the policy rather than the policy itself. Rules have a way of taking on a life of their own! It's easy to shift focus from supporting the mission and goals of the program to making people comply with the rules without thinking about why the rules exist. Work with the parents to figure out what the child's need is, and try to find a way to address it.

Avoid making judgments about parents' concerns or disagreements with policies. To imply that you know what is better for a child than his parents is likely to offend them. Explain the difference between what is successful at home and what works well in your program setting. You may have strong feelings about toy weapons and young children, but families who hunt or work for the Department of Defense may have different values. It will be less offensive to these parents if you say, "We find classroom management easier if we don't allow toy weapons," rather than, "We believe that playing with toy weapons is bad for children and encourages aggression."

Understand that parents' first concerns are for their child's happiness. It is unreasonable to expect parents to place as much importance on making the class runs smoothly or keeping things fair for the other children as they do on improving their own child's experience. Help parents see how a policy makes a better, happier learning experience for their child.

Ask for parents' help in developing policies that will work for teachers and families. This can be done formally or informally. I have always had an advisory committee of parents and community members to review policies and to help invent them. Not only do they come up with great ideas, but it is easier for parents to buy into rules when they have a voice. When parents wanted to change a policy, this group provided a forum for them to be heard. Here is an example: a parent wanted us to change our policy of allowing only adults to sign out children from the center. This parent wanted her thirteen-year-old daughter to get off the school bus at our center and walk her younger sister home. I was not comfortable with allowing this exception to the policy and suggested the parent make her case to the committee. Committee members asked questions including these: What if there were a lightning storm—who would get your children home then? What if your children were followed home by a stranger? In the end, the committee did not recommend rescinding the policy, but the parent left feeling that her request had been given serious consideration.

Ask parents for feedback on policies and take their answers into consideration for revision. I used a questionnaire that went out to all parents each year, and I had an exit survey. Parents were given a chance to reflect on their experiences, and we learned from their experience at the center.

When Nothing Seems to Work

What should you do if families refuse to follow policies? Generally, teachers are quick to want families tossed out of schools when they are caught in power struggles. By nature we tend to be people who don't enjoy conflict—that's why we didn't go to law school! At times, conflict is so uncomfortable that we want to move quickly to sever the relationship, but that shouldn't always be our first option. Honestly, the best experience I ever had working with parents was in a program where making families leave wasn't an option because the program was publicly funded. We all knew we had to work things out, and it made us very creative problem solvers! In many ways, it was a relief to have the option of asking the family to leave taken off the table.

Asking families to leave should always be a last resort. Here are some guidelines for taking action when you have come to a stalemate:

1. Decide if the issue is important enough to lose a child in your program. Once you have locked into a power struggle, parents may withdraw their child from the program. Situations that may warrant severe reactions include these:
   - The safety of children is involved.
   - If not following school policy places children in danger, you may be unable to avoid conflict.
   - There are legal consequences for you.
   - If parents are ignoring policies that are mandated (signing in and out, for instance), you cannot place yourself and your program in jeopardy.
   - The lack of parental compliance escalates.
   - Sometimes people have issues with authority and rules. If parents are unable to accept that you need to set some parameters, the power struggle may never end. You can put your foot down now, or you can put your foot down later.
   - The lack of compliance has a negative effect on other families.
   - In most programs, families are aware of what the others do and say. If you are making an exception to rules that you cannot justify to yourself, what will you say to other parents when they ask? You may need to take a stand to keep resentment from growing among the other families.

2. If you want to keep the family in the program, you can try the following:
   - Ask the parents for help in finding a solution.
   - If they realize how critical this issue is for you, they may have an idea you didn't think of.
   - Share the issue (confidentially) with other professionals.

- Chat rooms, such as NAEYC's Members Only website, are wonderful resources. You can get ideas from asking participating teachers how they have handled such issues.
- Examine the match between your own values and those of the school.
- Sometimes it is the teacher who is not on the same page as the rest of the school community. If a policy is much more important to you than it is to others, you may be in the wrong school.

New and Emerging Issues: Social Media Policies

A teacher recently shared with me that her school was working to develop a social media policy. It came up because a disgruntled parent shared negative comments about the school, specific teachers, and her feelings about other parents and children on Facebook. The school was unsure how to handle the situation in the absence of written policies. Consider creating school policies related to certain areas of social media:

- policies regarding staff and parents as social media "friends"
- policies on discussing the school on network sites
- policies on the use of photos taken at the school on social network sites

While these are challenging policies to enforce, without written policies staff's and parents' expectations are unclear.

Ideas for enforcing these policies include the following:

- providing written policies at time of enrollment and requiring parents to sign a commitment to following the policies
- providing clear consequences for not following policies, such as first a warning, then expulsion from school

SCENARIO 6

SCENARIO

Parents Who Don't Follow School Rules, or "But we're special!"

You can hear Sally's frustration:

"We have a clearly stated policy: No toys from home. It's in our parent handbook. When kids bring toys from home, parents blame us if they become lost or broken. Kids end up fighting over toys all the time, which takes away from the activities we set up for them. Tasha keeps bringing these stupid McDonald's toys. All the kids get excited, and she controls the whole class while she decides who gets to hold it. Someone ends up in tears, and I have to take the toy away. I have brought this up to her mother repeatedly. I am ready to frisk her when she enters school."

Tasha's mom is also frustrated:

"I don't know why the teacher has to be so uptight about toys from home. It is so hard to get my daughter to leave for school in the morning, and taking a toy with her makes it so much easier. I don't care if it is lost or broken. Tasha says she understands that she is taking a risk, and I don't let her bring anything important anyway. It just makes things so much easier for us. I think the school could be flexible about this. They want flexibility from us, don't they?"

WHAT IS THE PROBLEM?

The main issue here for the teacher is usually control over the classroom's environment and emotional climate. The teacher wants to choose what equipment is available for children. The parent does not see it this way—home toys and school toys are just toys. She wants her child to be happy to go to school.

Sometimes parents may want to change the program and learning environment you have created. If they send workbooks, phonics videos, and other teaching tools, it may be a signal that they do not understand (or accept) your educational philosophy.

WHAT ARE YOU THINKING?

Be aware of how your reaction might make the situation worse. Moving toward positive solutions is easier if you can recognize and avoid certain defensive mindsets that can make it difficult to develop a healthy partnership with parents. Typical defensive reactions include these:

"The parent doesn't respect my authority." You may think the parents are purposely defying school policy, while the parents may think that the policy is a suggestion rather than a rule.

"Toys from home encourage commercialism and competition between children." Remember that parents are not likely to observe the subtle changes that occur in your classroom in reaction to toys.

"Toys from home take the focus away from my curriculum." It is frustrating to work hard developing plans for classroom activities that are usurped by other activities that you see as having little value. Remember, parents experience the dynamic interest of their children rather than focusing on one interest or topic at a time. They aren't going to be as invested in your daily or weekly curriculum plan as you are.

"Other educators and parents will think badly of me if I have Barbies (or weapons, Disney toys, or coloring books) in my classroom." You are proud of the environment you create and want to be judged by what you intend rather than by what others bring into the environment. This is especially challenging in high-visibility sites, such as lab schools. Try to keep your ego out of the equation. Remember that being flexible in order to meet the needs of families and children is just as much of a philosophical rock to stand on as developmentally appropriate practice is.

WHAT ARE PARENTS THINKING?

Thinking about how our actions strike emotional chords with parents (just as their actions have an impact on us) can help us to be more sensitive.

"The teacher thinks I'm a bad parent for letting my daughter have this toy." Parents feel judged if they get the impression that you think their children's toys are inappropriate. Toy choices are values choices. Toy guns, toy makeup, fashion-model dolls, and flash cards reflect values. It is critical to be sensitive in this situation. For example, toy weapons can be as much a part of life as other pretend items.

"I saved for a long time to give my child this toy, and the teacher doesn't even care." Parents with limited resources may be very proud of a fancy doll or other expensive toy their child has. Your lack of acceptance of it in the classroom may feel hurtful.

"The teachers have to say, 'No toys,' but I don't think they really care as long as I don't fuss if it gets lost." Some cultures base their communication on negotiation more than others do. Some families may think that a rule is a starting place, and practice depends on personal negotiations. What seems like good bargaining to them may feel like a challenge to you.

"The teacher wants my child to be just like her kids." Trust can also be an issue if there is a difference between the cultural values of the family and your own values. Parents may correctly assume that you do not share their values for their children (such as expectations for compliance, problem solving, or checking aggression), so they may be looking for those values to collide.

SOLVING THE PROBLEM

Each situation will require unique solutions, but the following are some paths you might take.

Put your own feelings aside. Read the list of defensive reactions (above) again. Pay attention to the ones you may be feeling. Do any of these make you grit your teeth or your heart beat faster? Take a deep breath and experiment with what would happen if you let go of these reactions.

Listen to the parent's description of his experience and feelings about this matter. Sometimes just knowing that you are heard is enough to encourage a person to start finding solutions. "Tell me about when you leave for school. Does taking the toy along make it easier?"

Be prepared for parents to sound tense, angry, or frustrated. This is probably even harder for them to deal with than it is for you. Even if they are hurtful or blaming, remember that the problem right now is the situation, not you.

Reflect back the parent's concern. This helps parents know that they have been heard. "It sounds like it is really tough to get Tasha going in the morning, and bringing a toy is the one thing that has been making it easier."

Share your experience of the child at school with the parent. It helps for the parent to know what effect the issue has on her child's happiness at school. "What I have seen is that the toy is making it harder for Tasha to enjoy her day at school. There is so much squabbling over the toy, Tasha spends most of playtime worrying about that and doesn't take part in all of the other activities we have here in the preschool. I hate to see her missing out."

Find a solution everyone is willing to try. Perhaps Tasha loves dogs. Maybe if you had some toy dogs in the block area, she wouldn't feel the need to bring her stuffed dogs from home. Maybe she wants her friends to see her toy, and bringing a photo or drawing of it will suffice. Maybe she needs to bring a piece of home with her to school to feel safe, and putting the toy up on a shelf or in her cubby until she leaves will be good enough. Maybe she just needs the reassurance of walking out the door of her home with something familiar and can leave it in the car with her parent.

AFTER THE PROBLEM IS SOLVED: MOVING TOWARD TRUE PARTNERSHIP

You can address each issue as it comes up, or you can stretch yourself and your policies to partner with families. The following are some ideas of places to start.

Work with parents to create policies. These policies should be based on a shared vision of a desirable classroom environment. At a parent meeting early in the year, have a brainstorming session about the physical and emotional atmosphere and how a good environment can be created.

Stay open to alternatives. For instance, well-known preschool teacher Bev Bos allows children to bring an item from home and drop it in a basket for "showing." At the appropriate time, children are invited to retrieve their item and can show it to a friend. This gives children the opportunity to show their friends toys from home without subjecting the class to the boring ritual of Show and Tell.

BEFORE YOU HAVE A PROBLEM

The following suggestions can be used to avoid problems when parents don't follow policies.

Give parents copies of policies. Have both parents read the policy? Maybe dad or mom didn't know toys were not allowed.

Write policies clearly. Is what is not allowed clear? Maybe parents think a learning game, such as a portable computer game, belongs to a different category than a toy.

Talk to parents about policies during enrollment. Go over this rule when the child enrolls. Parents have a lot to focus on when reading through a parent handbook, and they may not have noticed a particular rule. Once children start bringing toys, it is more uncomfortable for everyone to change the routine.

Compromise and stay flexible whenever possible. If you aren't willing to consider alternatives, you are missing an opportunity to model problem solving in child rearing for the parents.

Avoid judgments about parents' concerns or disagreements with policies. Think about the language you use in your policies. "Superheroes and other violent toys" is a judgment. Some people think that superheroes are good role models for children.

Understand parents' concern for their child's happiness. Making their child cry to abide by a rule they don't understand or agree with isn't going to feel okay to most parents.

Fear of Health Problems Part 1, or The Sun Devil

Emma thinks that Kenny's mom is overreacting:

"Mrs. Keller told us that Kenny is sensitive to the sun and that he should wear a hat outdoors. That's fine, but I don't want to be the Hat Police. She said he doesn't mind wearing the hat, but I should remind him. I always make sure he puts it on before we go on the playground, but it tends to fall off. I want children to be physically active. Kenny isn't the most coordinated kid. If he is worrying about his hat, he's not paying attention to climbing and running. The other day, Mrs. Keller came when we were on the playground, and she just went off on me about Kenny not wearing his hat. Doesn't she realize I have nineteen other children to think about? I need to make sure no one really gets hurt outdoors. Making Kenny wear his hat is not my first priority."

For Mrs. Keller, it is a very big deal:

"I don't know why Kenny's teacher won't have him wear his hat! He is only three years old and can't be expected to know he has to wear a hat. My dad died of skin cancer, and Kenny is predisposed to have sun sensitivity. I bought him a hat he likes just for day care. I don't have any trouble getting him to wear his hat at home, but when the kids are outside when I pick Kenny up, he never has his hat on! How hard can it be? I can't go to work and keep my mind on my job if I think that Kenny isn't getting what he needs."

SCENARIO 7

WHAT IS THE PROBLEM?

Health issues cut to the core of parenting. What makes parents fearful may be less related to actual danger and more related to past experiences. You cannot talk a parent out of a health-related fear unless you are a physician or mental health counselor. This is true for fears related to allergies, exposure to communicable disease, and injury. The best you can do is to be flexible when you can, and be clear about limits when changes would have a negative effect on your program.

If a parent is upset because a child experiences a health-related problem at school or the parent perceives that you have placed the child at risk, information and levelheadedness are the most valuable ways of keeping the problem from escalating.

Document, document, document! It is very upsetting to be second-guessed when you believe you acted appropriately in a crisis. Keeping records of what happened will serve you. Sometimes parents seem accepting about an event and days later appear angry or accusing about the actions taken. This may be a function of the parent's initial relief that nothing worse happened, then reconsidering later; or sometimes the other parent has a different reaction when hearing about the same event.

WHAT ARE YOU THINKING?

Be aware of how your reaction might make the situation worse. Moving toward positive solutions is easier if you can recognize and avoid certain defensive mindsets that can make it difficult to develop a healthy partnership with parents. Typical defensive reactions include these:

"This parent doesn't trust me!" When a parent fears for her child's safety, even a spouse may be scrutinized. It is not about you—it's about the child.

"This parent's demands will keep me from being able to perform my job for the other children." Remember that it isn't reasonable to expect parents to care as much about the well-being of other children as the well-being of their own child.

"What if something really bad happens?" The possibility of a child being injured in some way while in group care is one of the risks of dealing with such a vulnerable population. Restricting your program to only healthy children without known problems won't keep you safe.

WHAT ARE PARENTS THINKING?

Thinking about how our actions strike emotional chords with parents (just as their actions have an impact on us) can help us to be more sensitive. Concerns over health are especially prevalent for families of children with special needs.

"The teacher isn't taking good care of my child." When a child experiences a serious illness, parents are often overwhelmed by a sense of powerlessness. They can become determined to keep anything bad from happening to their child again. Children with chronic health problems can have stronger reactions to seemingly innocuous exposures, such as common childhood diseases or insect bites, than other children and may require greater vigilance.

"The teacher isn't telling me what is really happening at school." Keep parents informed about near misses. Your initial reaction to a crisis avoided (such as a child almost receiving the wrong dose of medicine at school or a child falling from a tree but landing on the grass) might be to want to put it out of your mind, but rumors have a way of spreading. If children tell their parents about an event, they are likely to get parts of it wrong. If parents have first heard about the event from you, they can fill in the blanks to the stories they hear from their child. Meet with a parent after an event to analyze what happened. Is it likely to happen again? Some problems are difficult to avoid (such as a birthday treat from home with ingredients that some children are allergic to). Having a plan for what will happen next time is valuable. It lets parents know that you understand their need to have a say in what happens to their child when out of their care. It also tells parents that you take the problem seriously enough to spend time talking about it.

SOLVING THE PROBLEM

Each situation will require unique solutions, but the following are some paths you might take.

Put your own feelings aside. This is not about you. Annoyance at having to keep track of a hat is not the same level of emotion as being afraid your child will contract skin cancer.

Listen to the parent's description of her experience and feelings about this matter. To resist defensiveness, keep your attention on the parent.

Be prepared for parents to sound tense, angry, or frustrated. Sometimes scared sounds like angry, so resist reacting to a parent's comments.

Reflect back the parent's concern. This is when you can really show the parent you get it. "It must be hard to live in this climate and worry about your son being in danger!"

Share your experience of the child at school with the parent. "I now understand the importance of Kenny wearing a hat, but I want to figure out a way for him to be really active at school. When he slows down because his hat is coming loose, he is not taking part in the active play that is so good for his motor development."

Find a solution everyone is willing to try. Can your group use the playground earlier in the day, when the sun is less intense? Can you find hats that stay on more easily? Would a hat that Kenny chose himself be easier for him to remember? Can you make Kenny feel part of the group by reading *Caps for Sale* and having hats available for everyone to use?

AFTER THE PROBLEM IS SOLVED: MOVING TOWARD TRUE PARTNERSHIP

You can address each issue as it comes up, or you can stretch yourself and your policies to partner with families. The following are places to start.

Invite parents to talk to each other. A buddy system for parents whose children have similar issues can be helpful and welcoming. If you have a child entering your program with peanut allergies, for example, ask a veteran family with peanut issues to call the new parents and talk to them—after getting the permission of both parents to ensure confidentiality.

Have parents perform an audit. Invite a parent of a child with health issues to evaluate how the program handles the issue, including policies, supplies, training, and so on. An audit can give you useful information and help create trust with the parent.

BEFORE YOU HAVE A PROBLEM

The following suggestions can be used to avoid problems when policies are creating strife between you and a parent.

Make program policies consistent with laws and rules that affect your program. If this child has a health issue, you may be obligated by the ADA to take all reasonable precautions to protect him from the sun. Be clear about your limits. For instance, if a child has an allergy, you may be able to exclude rabbits from a particular classroom but unable to ban rabbits from the entire school.

Tell parents about policies before enrollment. Talk to parents before children enroll in your program about their concerns. Ask lots of questions to be sure you understand their level of concern. "Do you want him wearing a hat even if it's cloudy?" Or for an allergic child: "If your child is stung by a bee, do you want us to call you even if she seems fine?" "What first aid are you expecting us to administer?" Have a plan for what will happen if the child has a health incident at school. Go beyond just filling out the emergency card. Talk to the parent about who should be called first, under what circumstances, and what should happen if you're on a field trip.

Compromise and stay flexible whenever possible. If it's going to be hard for a child to walk on a windy day while wearing a hat, make a plan with the parent for alternative sun protection. Use clear language. Avoid words such as "rarely," "occasionally," and "often." They mean different things to different people. Try to use numbers (twice a week, once a day) so parents know what you mean.

Avoid judgments about parents' concerns or disagreements with politics. It is not up to you to determine if this child is truly in danger. That is the task of his parents and doctors.

Understand parents' concern for their child's happiness. Try to make it easy for parents to insist on consistency between home and school. It is possible to give a child the unintended message that you don't think he should have to follow his mother's rule.

Fear of Health Problems Part 2, or Typhoid Mary

Betsy is feeling defensive:

"Everyone knows that part of being in preschool is getting colds and other bugs. We have rules, and the parents basically follow them, but kids still get sick. Most of the parents are really understanding about it, but Mrs. Lewis gets really upset. She only sends her son to child care on Tuesdays, and she calls every Wednesday to say he is sick again, as if it's our fault. I don't know what she expects us to do!"

Mrs. Lewis has her own perspective:

"I do my best to keep my son out of child care because I know how sick kids get. Relatives watch him almost every day, but I have to send him in on Tuesdays. Every time I drop him off, I see kids with runny noses who are coughing and just not looking healthy. I tell my son to stay away from them, but he always gets sick. I don't know if they won't make parents keep their kids home because they don't want to lose the money, or what. I think it would help if they kept the place cleaner too. I wouldn't worry so much, but he always has ear infections, and the pediatrician says it will affect his language development."

WHAT IS THE PROBLEM?

Having a sick child turns a parent's life upside down. Parents worry about their children and hate seeing them uncomfortable. Alternate child care arrangements must be made, or parents must miss work. Children who don't feel well tend to not sleep well, and this affects parents' sleep. On top of all this, add fear about how infections can affect children's development and guilt over placing a child in harm's way if child care is where the child gets sick. Even if children are not picking up illnesses at school, parents are likely to assume the school is the culprit.

Once parents have become upset over exposure to illness, remind them of your health and safety practices. Listen to their frustrations with patience. If they have suggestions for improving your policies, listen politely so they will feel heard. Sincerely saying, "Those are some interesting ideas. I'll give them some thought," doesn't commit you to anything.

If policies have not been followed, let the parent know that you are aware of what happened and that steps will be taken to ensure that it won't happen again.

WHAT ARE YOU THINKING?

Be aware of how your reaction might make the situation worse. Moving toward positive solutions is easier if you can recognize and avoid certain defensive mindsets that can make it difficult to develop a healthy partnership with parents. Typical defensive reactions include these:

"This parent doesn't think the school is clean." People have different standards for sanitation, and you are likely to have some parents in the program who would prefer a more hospital-like level of cleanliness. It isn't about you as a person.

"This parent will say bad things about the program to her pediatrician, and we'll get a bad reputation." Most doctors understand the issues of exposure in group child care.

"This parent expects me to handle her child with kid gloves." Keeping conflict with parents from interfering with your relationship with the child is critical. Resist the urge to pull away from the child emotionally.

WHAT ARE PARENTS THINKING?

Thinking about how our actions strike emotional chords with parents (just as their actions have an impact on us) can help us to be more sensitive.

"My child is going to pick up something terrible!" Some cultures fuss over health more than others.

"How can I afford to take her to the doctor again?" Parents with limited access to health care may be especially concerned about illness.

SCENARIO 8

"I'm going to miss work again. I hope I don't lose my job!" Parents in minimum-wage jobs or jobs without benefits are hurt by loss of pay when they must stay home with a sick child.

SOLVING THE PROBLEM

Each situation will require unique solutions, but the following are some paths you might take.

Put your own feelings aside. Parents don't have as much experience with typical childhood illnesses as most teachers. We may groan when we have a lice outbreak, but for parents, it can be exhausting and humiliating.

Reflect back the parent's concern. "It sounds like taking your child to the doctor means a long bus ride and a day's pay lost. I can see how hard that is."

Share your experience of the child at school with the parent. "I know it's scary when your child has a fever. But when you keep her home because you are afraid she might get sick, it's hard for her to develop relationships with the other children. Adjustment has to start all over again."

Find a solution everyone is willing to try. I worked with several children who were undergoing chemotherapy. It was always a delicate balance trying to limit their exposure to illness and ensure a consistent school experience. These children's parents were willing to write a note to the other parents in the class. They asked the other parents to call them at home if their child had been exposed to something that would not be serious for a healthy child but placed their children with compromised immune systems in jeopardy. The other parents were happy to comply and also tended to be more cautious about sending a sick child to school.

AFTER THE PROBLEM IS SOLVED: MOVING TOWARD TRUE PARTNERSHIP

You can address each issue as it comes up, or you can stretch yourself and your policies to partner with families. The following are some places to start.

Invite a public health nurse to a parent meeting. A public health nurse could inform parents about disease exposure in child care settings.

Invite parents to take part in an audit. Ask parents to help evaluate your health and safety policies and procedures and to make suggestions for improvement.

Encourage parents to spend time in the program. When parents realize how participating in the program benefits their child, they may be less concerned about the occasional cold.

BEFORE YOU HAVE A PROBLEM

The following suggestions can be used to avoid problems when health policies are a concern for parents.

Make program policies consistent with laws and rules that affect your program. Most programs are licensed by a state agency, and rules about contagious diseases are usually included. National Association for the Education of Young Children (NAEYC) accreditation also addresses this topic. Make sure your policies are consistent with these rules as well as with the best current pediatric health information. Be sure that the staff is using sound health practices. Have all children and adults wash their hands as soon as they enter the building. This can help keep germs out. Teach adults and children sanitary hand-washing procedures, including using a paper towel to turn off the faucet to guard against picking up germs that have been left behind. Sanitize toys often. Avoid sharing bottles or food.

Give parents copies of policies. Giving parents a separate flyer to keep at home that explains when children must stay home from school is often helpful. Parents aren't likely to think about rashes or lice until they experience those issues. Be clear about refund policies for when children miss school. You don't want to have an argument with a parent who is already stressed out over having a sick child.

Write policies clearly. When must a child be kept at home? Make sure the policy is specific (for example, a "temperature of over 100 degrees") rather than general ("has a fever").

Make consequences of not following policies clear. What happens if a child comes to school sick? What happens if a child does not attend school regularly? Spell it out.

Tell parents about policies before enrollment. Help parents understand that their children are taking part in a larger germ pool by attending school. Point out that they can either expose their children to typical childhood germs now or wait until their children enter elementary school, when absence from school will affect their children's academic experience differently.

When they first enroll, talk to parents about arrangements for children who become ill during the school day. Have a specific location for isolating sick children. Include a system for notifying parents if children need to be picked up from school. Make sure you also have the names of people besides the parents who can pick up children. If the backups are out of town or unavailable, you may be stuck until pickup time. Send out notices of exposure. While it might seem overwhelming to tell every parent about every exposure, they usually appreciate having a heads-up.

Compromise and stay flexible whenever possible. Hear what parents would like you to do to cut back on exposures, and consider their suggestions.

Avoid judgments about parents' concerns or disagreements with policies. A simple cold may seem like no big deal to you, but it can have a huge effect on a family, ranging from lost sleep to lost work and medical bills.

Understand parents' concerns for their children's happiness. A parent is naturally going to be most concerned with his own child's health. Saying to a parent, "I know that other child has a nasty cough, but he's missed so much school, I just hated to send him home again," will not be an acceptable response for most parents.

Develop relationships. Encourage parents to spend time in the program. When parents realize the benefits of their child taking part in the program, they may be less concerned about the occasional cold.

The Parent Who Won't Leave, or "How can I miss you when you won't say good-bye?"

Tommy's teacher is ready for Tommy's mom to move on:

"Tommy's mom is making him miserable! She just won't leave! We have a whole routine of two kisses and two hugs; then I hold his hand when Mom leaves. She just keeps prolonging it. He cries, and she comes back. We start the whole cycle over again. She leaves and realizes she forgot to check his cubby. Or she decides she has to tell me something. Each time she comes back, he gets upset all over again. This keeps me tied up for an hour every morning, and it's time I can't spend with the other children."

Tommy's mom is struggling:

"It's just so hard to leave Tommy. I try to put on a happy face, and I begin each morning telling him how much fun he is going to have at school. But then we get there, and when I try to leave, he cries and cries. His teacher just expects me to leave him crying. It's too hard! I don't want him to feel abandoned. I know it's taking a long time, but he is just too upset. You can tell she isn't a parent and doesn't know how it feels to leave your child crying."

WHAT IS THE PROBLEM?

Separation is a huge deal for parents. While we as teachers have seen children making this transition every year and can predict how long it's going to take, it is a very new and personal issue for some parents. Guilt over leaving the child, fear of leaving the child in the wrong hands, fear of losing the child's love and trust, sadness at missing one's child, and personal issues of abandonment and loss all play into the intensity. By bullying parents to move through this issue at our pace, we risk forcing the parents to sabotage their adjustment efforts or to give up some of their self-image as parents. Neither is good for children.

WHAT ARE YOU THINKING?

Be aware of how your reaction might make the situation worse. Moving toward positive solutions is easier if you can recognize and avoid certain defensive mind-sets that can make it difficult to develop a healthy partnership with parents. Typical defensive reactions include these:

"If I let the child manipulate me, he will be less compliant." While it is important for children to accept routines and limits, separation anxiety is real (Balaban 1985). Very few children use it for manipulation. If you stop questioning the sincerity of the child's feelings, it is easier to find a good solution.

"If I let the parent break the rules, she won't accept my authority." The best way to avoid this issue is to avoid inflexible rules.

"I am losing control of my classroom with all of these parents hanging around." Some teachers thrive in an environment full of adults. Others are overwhelmed by having many bodies and personalities in the classroom. You can adjust your schedule so that serious things happen after the parents leave. I have also set limits for parents if I felt they were becoming their children's school playmates and interfering with their children adjusting to the teacher and other children. I have said, "You need to be present so your child feels secure, but not interesting enough so she depends on you to navigate the classroom. Be boring. Sit in the same chair. Bring a magazine or some work." I have then slowly moved the chair toward the classroom door, into the hall, into the entryway, and eventually out the door.

"The other parents are going to think they should stay too." You can reassure other parents that their children are fine with them leaving.

"The parent must think I can't handle her child." This is probably not the case. If it is, you can help the parent change her mind by observing you with other children.

"The parent is going to observe me doing things he won't approve of." Most parents in this situation will be so focused on their own child that they won't judge you. There is a risk that the parent will observe things he doesn't understand and report information to other parents. All you can do is trust other parents to read through the situation.

"The child will never bond with me." Take steps to develop a rapport with the child. Don't depend on the parent to handle her child in the classroom, and the bonding will happen faster.

"I am spending so much time with this child, the other children aren't getting my attention." In general, all of the children in the group are relieved that you are caring for an anxious friend, and they are not jealous. If you find that the separation transition is taking so long that it is interfering with your interactions with other children, you can arrange for parents to let you know when they are ready for help leaving. You can focus on the other children until then.

WHAT ARE PARENTS THINKING?

Thinking about how our actions strike emotional chords with parents (just as their actions have an impact on us) can help us to be more sensitive.

"This teacher doesn't understand how my people feel about a mother leaving her child." Separation is a culturally sensitive issue. It is important that you understand the cultural norms of the groups you serve. Are mothers supposed to stay with their children? They may not say this to you, in an attempt to fit in with the dominant culture, but mothers may be torn between your expectation that they leave and their own culture's expectation that they stay with their children. If you expect more independence from children than their culture demands, mothers may feel that their children will not be properly cared for. Examples include expectations for self-feeding and being carried by an adult after a child is able to walk on his or her own.

"The teacher doesn't understand how boys are supposed to act." Expectations may be different for boys than for girls. If boys are expected not to cry, it may be difficult for a parent to leave their male child in tears. Differences in the expectations that fathers and mothers have can also create a lack of consistency and add to adjustment difficulties.

"The teacher's wrong. I'm just going to do what is right for my child." Communication styles are an issue. Parents may not approve of the separation policy and may not tell you. In some cultures it is rude to disagree with people. So parents may verbally agree to an action but not follow through.

"The teacher says he stops crying as soon as I leave, but how can I be sure?" Trust is an issue. If you are different from a family in culture, language, or in other ways, you may not be trusted to care for their children once they leave. Parents bring their own childhood experiences into their roles as parents. If a parent is not allowed to use his native language in school or if he experiences favoritism of one group over another, it may take a while for you to earn his trust.

SOLVING THE PROBLEM

Each situation will require unique solutions, but the following are some paths you might take.

Put your own feelings aside. Once you find yourself in a power struggle with a parent about leaving the classroom, stop before it escalates and have a meeting. Make a plan together.

Listen to the parent's description of her experience and feelings. Evaluate the present situation. Listen to the parent. While she may feel she is making progress with her child or she says, "This is how it always is when I leave," you may find the situation is detrimental to the child or the other children.

Share your experience of the child at school with the parent. Share what you are seeing in an objective way. Saying, "You never leave," is emotionally loaded. Try, "You say good-bye and then stay for ten to twenty minutes." Saying, "Each time you come back, Tommy cries and has a bad day," is guilt inducing. Try, "Tommy takes up to an hour before he joins an activity, and he wakes up from nap crying."

Find a solution everyone is willing to try. Get some history. How has the child dealt with separation? What was traumatic? What went easily? Brainstorm some ideas with the parent. Make a plan that you can both live with. Compromise may be required. You may think it would be easier if the parent brought the child to school earlier, when there are fewer children for you to attend to. If she is not able or willing to do this, you need to move on to a new idea. Ask the parent to describe what the ideal scenario would look like to her. Would the child run into the classroom and not look back? Would he hug mom and then turn to the arms of his teacher? Find out if you both have the same image so you can have a common goal. Plan a script together. Come up with signals that show the parent is ready for you to take the child from her arms. It will be easiest for the child to see you working as a united front.

Decide together what success will look like. Prepare the parent for setbacks. Try to get a commitment to work on a plan over a period of time. Let the parent know that regression is common, especially if circumstances change—such as a parent going out of town or having a substitute teacher at school. Celebrate small steps toward success. When the parent can leave for a portion of the day, that's a step. When the child stops crying a few minutes after the parent leaves, that's a step.

AFTER THE PROBLEM IS SOLVED: MOVING TOWARD TRUE PARTNERSHIP

You can address each issue as it comes up, or you can stretch yourself and your policies to partner with families. The following are some places to start:

- Create a good-bye window or other physical place for families to separate.
- Provide parents with a way to view their children that is out of sight, such as a two-way mirror or a video camera they can check from work.
- Send parents a text with a short video of their child happily engaged in play.

BEFORE YOU HAVE A PROBLEM

The following suggestions can be used to avoid problems when parents are struggling with separation anxiety.

Make program policies consistent with laws and rules that affect your program. When laws do not address this issue, you can still look to best practices in the early childhood education (ECE) field. Will you have different rules for different ages of children? Do you expect the same from parents of infants and toddlers as you do for those of preschoolers or schoolagers? Think through policies for their developmental appropriateness.

Write policies clearly. How long are you willing to let parents stay? It can be helpful to state upfront how long you will proceed with a plan and when you will review it together. This keeps you from sticking with a plan that is obviously not working and sets the tone that you will work through issues with the parent as a team.

Make clear the consequences of not following policies. What is your bottom line with separation? At what point is it not working? If parents do not follow policies regarding separation and adjustment to school, will their child be disenrolled? If a child needs to withdraw from the program, can the family get a refund? These issues matter to families.

Another way to think about this is whether you believe someone is to blame if a child does not make a successful transition into your program. When I was a young teacher, I had an insightful parent say to me after a couple of weeks of trying to get her son to separate, "Right now, Matthew is an oval peg and school is a round hole. I feel like if I pushed and prodded hard enough, I'd get him in the space, but it won't be comfortable or natural. Let's wait another year and see what shape he takes." She was absolutely right, and the next year he made an easy transition. Fortunately, she had the luxury of allowing him another year before starting school.

Talk to parents about policies at enrollment. How do you define successful separation and adjustment? Talk to the parents before enrollment. They may expect that their child will not cry, and the situation won't seem successful to them until they can leave with no tears. They may expect the child to be engaged in play before they leave. This can lead to a vicious cycle of a parent coaxing their child to engage in activity only to find that he disengages when they attempt to leave. They may expect the child to choose when they leave and won't leave until the child approves the move. This places too much responsibility on the child.

Compromise and stay flexible whenever possible. Have a policy that provides flexibility for different situations and individuals. A flexible policy will be easiest to enforce and the most useful in the long run.

Avoid judgments about parents' concerns or disagreements with policies. Teachers often make this comment: "It's not the child who is having a hard time. His mom is just encouraging him to cry!" For young children, the connection between parent and child is so strong that the origin of the concern doesn't matter.

Understand parents' concern for their children's happiness. Share information, such as the NAEYC brochure "So Many Goodbyes" by Janet Brown McCracken, so parents know they are not alone.

Develop a relationship. Acknowledging the challenges of separation is a good place to start developing a partnership. Encourage supportive parents to help each other by planning to arrive at school at the same time so children can walk in with a buddy.

The Late Parent, or "Is it 6:15 already?"

Dora has had it!

"Mimi's dad is always late. I've tried to be subtle, looking at the clock a lot, saying, 'Oh, Mimi, your dad is finally here!' But he doesn't get the hint. When he finally does come, she is so wound up from waiting for him that she runs around the room, making him chase her. Then they play this game while I am trying to leave! It's bad enough he is ten minutes late, but then by the time he gets her, signs her out, gets stuff out of her cubby, has her go potty one more time, it's more like a half hour. My director says she can't charge him when he is just ten minutes late, but I am getting out of work a half hour late every night!"

Mimi's father has a totally different read on the situation:

"Mimi's teacher doesn't seem to care much about her work. She just seems to care about punching the clock and leaving. I've tried chatting with her when I pick up Mimi, but she's not very friendly. It's my only opportunity to see what Mimi's school is like, since her mom drops her off in the morning. I never hear about Mimi's day, and if I try to read notices on the parent bulletin board or look at the kids' artwork, the teacher tries to get me to leave."

WHAT IS THE PROBLEM?

For many parents, the program's closing time means the time they need to get there. If a store closes at 5:00 p.m., they will still let you shop and ring you out as long as you get in the door on time. Parents may feel guilty about the long hours they are away from their children and want to show an interest in their classroom when they arrive. It may not occur to them that the teacher is anxious to leave. This can be especially challenging for parents to understand if they have jobs without set hours.

WHAT ARE YOU THINKING?

Be aware of how your reaction might make the situation worse. Moving toward positive solutions is easier if you can recognize and avoid certain defensive mindsets that can make it difficult to develop a healthy partnership with parents. Typical defensive reactions include these:

"This parent thinks I am his personal babysitter." You may feel marginalized by families who seem oblivious to your need to leave work on time. But a parent who does not adhere to pickup time may have any of a number of explanations, so don't personalize her tardiness.

"If I let them come late without consequences, they'll continue to take advantage of me." For some of us, standing up for our own rights can be difficult. Have faith that you and the parent can solve the problem together. The parent is probably not deliberately taking advantage of you.

"These parents think they are above the rules." You may be frustrated by watching some parents work so hard to get to school on time while others seem not to bother. Try not to make generalizations that will have a negative impact on your relationships.

WHAT ARE PARENTS THINKING?

Thinking about how our actions strike emotional chords with parents (just as their actions have an impact on us) can help us to be more sensitive.

"Why is this teacher so uptight about time?" Time is a concept bound by culture. While stereotypes about ethnic groups being late are disrespectful, adherence to the clock is a Western concept. Instead of assuming negative reasons for parents being habitually late, it is helpful to think instead of a different notion of what "on time" might mean.

"The teacher is just tidying up her classroom, why is it a problem if my child stays a little longer?" Don't expect parents to understand that you would not be there late tidying up the classroom if they had picked up their children on time—they won't understand this if you don't tell them.

SCENARIO 10

SOLVING THE PROBLEM

Each situation will require unique solutions, but the following are some paths you might take:

Put your own feelings aside. Keep the issue from clouding your relationship with the family. It is easy for a single frustration like this to become the center of the relationship between you and a parent. The biggest loser is the child. This is not the child's fault and is probably just one aspect of the interaction between the school and parent.

Listen to the parent's description of his experience and feelings about this matter. You may find that he is struggling with pickup time as much as you are.

Reflect back the parent's concern. "It sounds like you can't get here with more than five minutes to spare, and then you don't get a chance to see the classroom."

Share your experience with the parent and how it affects the child at school. Help the parent understand the consequence for his child. "When Ethan is the last child to get picked up, he gets anxious. I know that isn't how you want to start your evening with him."

Find a solution everyone is willing to try. You can brainstorm with parents to find a solution. Include suggesting a carpool with another family, having the family hire a teaching assistant to stay late with the child, or meeting the family in the parking lot with the child. If you take the position of partnering with the family to solve this problem rather than taking an adversarial position, you will win the cooperation of the family in other matters.

Have children ready to go. If parents have to spend ten minutes finding their children's shoes, you are going to get out even later. Having children all ready is another signal that it is time to go. Help parents out the door. Sometimes children react to waiting for late parents by trying to make their parents wait for them. Help parents herd their children out, assuring them that there will be time to show their work or finish that game tomorrow.

AFTER THE PROBLEM IS SOLVED: MOVING TOWARD TRUE PARTNERSHIP

You can address each issue as it comes up, or you can stretch yourself and your policies to partner with families. The following are some places to start.

Find out what parents need. Maybe polling parents will tell you that they need you to add more hours to your program.

Find out about transportation services. Some communities have bus services that parents can use.

BEFORE YOU HAVE A PROBLEM

The following suggestions can be used to avoid problems with chronically late parents.

Give parents copies of policies. Be clear about expectations for pickup. It is helpful to have the information in several places, such as in the parent handbook, on posters in the classroom, and in notes sent home. If Dad usually picks up, Mom may not know what pickup time is.

Make policies. Don't give double messages. If parents apologize for being late and you tell them, "No big deal," they are less likely to rush next time. Be polite but clear about the need for them to arrive on time.

Clearly state the consequences of not following policies. Have a policy in place that deters late pickup. Most programs have a late fee. If possible, involve an administrator in the issue so it does not turn into a power struggle between you and the parent. You might waive the fee the first time it happens and state, "This time we'll waive the fee, but next time we'll have to charge you." This way parents leave feeling relieved and understand the consequence for being late.

Pay attention to the details. Make sure clocks in the school are synchronized and accurate. The issue may be differing watches.

The Parent Who Wants Special Treatment, or "If it's not too much trouble . . ."

Antonia doesn't understand this parent's expectations:

"Ryan's mom always wants something special. He can't eat our hot lunches because the family is vegetarian. I respect that. But she brings food she wants us to heat up for him. That means I have to leave the classroom to use the microwave in the kitchen. Other teachers who are on break are heating up their own lunches, so I have to wait for them to finish. In the meantime, I have left my teaching assistant alone in the classroom to help all the other children with lunch. I've asked the mom to bring food that doesn't have to be heated, and she'll do that for a couple of days, but then we are back to the microwave again."

Ryan's mom is focused on her son's experience:

"It is hard for Ryan to be the only one in his class who eats different food. You should see the garbage they feed the kids—hot dogs and other foods full of chemicals and all kinds of things. I explained that we are vegetarians and we would bring food for Ryan each day when I enrolled him. The administration said I still had to pay the same tuition and I agreed, so they are making money on us. His teacher wants us to send cheese sandwiches every day so her life is easier, but I want Ryan to feel like the other kids. I look at their menu and try to fix him something similar, like veggie burgers. The other kids are getting hot food—why shouldn't Ryan?"

WHAT IS THE PROBLEM?

You may view the eating habits of the family as a choice, and the family does not see it as a choice. Food issues are not that different from other diversity issues. If you are Christian in a majority-Christian culture, you may not notice how many holidays and events are based on Christian culture. If you are not Christian, you are always aware of when your religious traditions are different from the majority culture. The same can be true for families who eat differently. While the teacher views the parent as making special demands, from the perspective of the parent, if all of the children were fed properly, it wouldn't be an issue. If a power struggle emerges over this issue, take a step back and focus on a solution that will work for everyone rather than trying to win.

WHAT ARE YOU THINKING?

Be aware of how your reaction might make the situation worse. Moving toward positive solutions is easier if you can recognize and avoid certain defensive mindsets that can make it difficult to develop a healthy partnership with parents. Typical defensive reactions include these:

"I am just supporting this parent's eccentricity." Diets can be based on religion, beliefs around health or politics (some people are vegetarians because it takes less land to grow vegetables than to feed cows), personal preference, or spiritual reasons (sometimes diets are designed by spiritual healers). If you try to judge a parent's reasons for making such choices, you are stepping over a line.

"If I give in to this, the parent will have a new demand." You don't want to be taken advantage of. Still, children are part of their families, and addressing families' needs is part of working well with children.

WHAT ARE PARENTS THINKING?

Thinking about how our actions strike emotional chords with parents (just as their actions have an impact on us) can help us to be more sensitive.

"The teacher doesn't support my decisions about my child." As stated above, religion or culture can dictate diet. Refusing to cooperate with these exceptions can signal a lack of tolerance for families' differences.

SCENARIO 11

"The teacher doesn't care about how my child feels." If a child is the only one who is not getting a hot lunch, he, as well as the parents, may experience a negative impact.

SOLVING THE PROBLEM

Each situation will require unique solutions, but the following are some paths you might take.

Be clear about the issue. If the parent's request is a problem, be clear about the issue. Is it a difficulty with accommodating a vegetarian? Is it bringing food from home? Is it preparing the food? The solution to the dilemma depends on why it is a problem. If you cannot accommodate a vegetarian, then you are not going to make your school inviting for people from some countries and cultures.

Find a solution everyone is willing to try. If leaving the room to prepare the food is the problem, maybe the parents can donate a microwave to your classroom. If the issue is bringing food from home, it might be time to look at your menu. If you come up with a solution (such as having the parents bring food that does not need heating) and the parents don't follow through, immediately contact them for a new solution. You can't let the child go hungry, but you can keep crackers and almond butter in your classroom and inform the parent you didn't have time to leave the room, so you substituted the food.

AFTER THE PROBLEM IS SOLVED: MOVING TOWARD TRUE PARTNERSHIP

You can address each issue as it comes up, or you can stretch yourself and your policies to partner with families. The following are places to start:

Show support for families who differ from the dominant culture. Include the needs of these families in school policies.

Why not serve only vegetarian food? Vegetarian meals won't hurt anyone and would be a great show of support for vegetarian families.

Find out if all the parents would be just as happy to send lunches from home. You may be jumping through hoops for no reason.

BEFORE YOU HAVE A PROBLEM

The following suggestions can be used to avoid problems with families with specific diets.

Make program policies consistent with laws and rules that affect your program. If your program receives subsidies from the United States Department of Agriculture, you must meet specific standards about what children are served in order to use those meals in your reimbursement counts. Menus need to be reevaluated every so often. We now have different standards for healthy diets than we did between the time the food pyramid came out and the new "My Plate," and some of us don't have enough whole grains in our menus.

Give parents copies of policies. Giving parents written menus and making sure to update menus gives parents a sense of security.

Write policies clearly. Make sure that explaining menu options is a part of the enrollment procedure so problems don't come up later. Menus must be clear. For instance, chili may have meat, beans, or both. Making recipes available for parents is helpful.

Compromise and stay flexible whenever possible. Establish similarities between home and school. When populations change (for example, families arrive from different countries), reevaluating the school lunches can be beneficial. Parents can be helpful in evaluating menu changes. Ask questions about food before the child begins. If parents have special requests, make a plan to honor their requests.

Avoid judgments about parents' concerns or disagreements with policies. Keep an open mind about the solution. Be aware of your own prejudices. I worked with one teacher who objected to a parent substituting a rice cake for the wheat crackers her child was allergic to, saying, "The rice cake is so big, it doesn't seem fair." Chances are, the other children are not going to care what the child eats if they know there is a reason.

SCENARIO
12

The Child with Special Needs, or "Why didn't you tell us?"

Eric is concerned:

"I always interview parents before they enroll their children to see if there is anything we should know. We even ask for developmental history. So Sean starts in my class, and I have no idea he has issues. Right away, I can tell something is wrong. During free play he is fine—he likes to use the blocks and finds a place where he can play without other children bothering him. But he hates cleanup time. When I sing the cleanup song, he gets excited, flapping his arms. I give him instructions, and he repeats back what I say. At first I tried physically moving him to the shelf to put away blocks. He started pushing me away and screaming. Now I just avoid the whole thing by letting him play with blocks through group time and snacktime. I don't know what else to do. I also feel angry with his mother for not telling me he was like this."

Sean's parent is trying to protect him:

"Sean's teacher is having a hard time working with him. He has always been sensitive, but as long as you tell him what is going to happen beforehand and keep to the same routine, he's fine. Lots of little kids are like that. His pediatrician said he is a little behind in some things, but I know he'll catch up. I thought this was a good school and they'd teach him how to behave. His last school asked him to leave because they weren't good with him. I didn't mention it to the new school because I didn't want him to start off on the wrong foot. Now I feel like his teacher doesn't like him."

WHAT IS THE PROBLEM?

Don't expect to get the whole picture from your first contact with families. The more challenging the child, the more likely parents will need to develop trust in you before divulging everything. Don't take it personally. If you do find yourself in the position of working with a child with special needs when you were not prepared to do so, move forward rather than focusing on what should have happened. Blame, second-guessing yourself, and resentment toward the family will just divert your energies from finding the best solution for the dilemma.

WHAT ARE YOU THINKING?

Be aware of how your reaction might make the situation worse. Moving toward positive solutions is easier if you can recognize and avoid certain defensive mindsets that can make it difficult to develop a healthy partnership with parents. Typical defensive reactions include these:

"I am going to get blamed for this child's problems." Especially in this time of accountability, it is easy to focus on covering your own tail instead of on what is best for the child. While documenting the behaviors you have observed and how you have responded is important in case questions come up, do not let that become your primary focus.

"What else is this parent withholding?" Regaining trust is hard once you feel as if you haven't been given all of the information you need.

WHAT ARE PARENTS THINKING?

Thinking about how our actions strike emotional chords with parents (just as their actions have an impact on us) can help us to be more sensitive.

"If my child has something wrong with him, he will have a terrible life." Different cultures respond to disabilities with more or less acceptance.

"My child will never be accepted." Understanding a disability's cultural implications for both parents is important. In-laws can also play a role in acceptance.

SOLVING THE PROBLEM

Each situation will require unique solutions, but the following are some paths you might take.

Put aside your own feelings. Stay focused on the present reality of the child's experience in school. It no longer matters that it would have been better if you had known beforehand. What is working for the child? What is overly challenging? What can help the child benefit from his school experience?

Let go of any negative feelings toward the parents. You need to form a team now.

Listen to the parents' description of their experience and feelings about this matter. Get parents in the classroom. It will help if they can see how their child behaves compared to other children before you have to describe the behavior. Know what resources you have access to. It helps to know about community resources and the resources the family has access to (such as health insurance).

Share your experience of the child at school with the parents. Make a plan to meet with them. Be clear that the focus is on what will best meet the child's needs.

Find a solution everyone is willing to try. Help parents move forward. Plan time and energy for working with the parents to improve their child's experiences. Be clear about your expectations. You will need the parents to follow through with decisions you make together. Look at creating forms of communication (such as written logs, e-mails, and phone calls), and set times for future meetings. Make a plan with the parents that moves on a continuum from least restrictive to most restrictive involvement. Target the most difficult times and events for the child. Is it during transitions? Try increasing support during transitions. Ask the director to help for fifteen minutes during the move from indoors to outdoors. Is it during field trips? Try having a family member come to help during field trips. If these less-restrictive solutions don't work, you can move toward more restrictive solutions, such as having parents pick up the child before rest time or keeping the child home when field trips are planned. Talk to the parents about having the child professionally assessed. Be prepared for hesitation on the part of the parents. We are all concerned about children's permanent records and labeling a child. While it is the responsibility of the public schools to provide screening and assessment of children ages three to twenty-one, public health facilities or private insurance carriers may offer alternatives. Acquiring this information can help you make the best plans for the child and may provide some outside resources for your program.

AFTER THE PROBLEM IS SOLVED: MOVING TOWARD TRUE PARTNERSHIP

You can address each issue as it comes up, or you can stretch yourself and your policies to partner with families. The following are places to start:

Become an inclusive setting. If you have a positive experience with including a child with special needs in your program, you may want to become an inclusive setting. This can be accomplished by partnering with other agencies to place children with special needs and offering the services they require.

Use Individual Education Plans (IEPs). Offer IEPs to all children in your center. It's a great way of ensuring individual appropriateness and includes families in setting goals for their children.

BEFORE YOU HAVE A PROBLEM

The following suggestions can be used to avoid problems with families whose children may have special needs.

Make program policies consistent with laws and rules that affect your program. Make sure you understand your legal obligations, especially in accordance with the ADA. Programs are expected to include children and parents with disabilities unless it would cause a "direct threat" to other children or "fundamental alteration" of the program. Programs are required to make "reasonable modifications" that don't cause "undue burden." For more information, you can read *Commonly Asked Questions about Child Care Centers and the Americans with Disabilities Act* (U.S. Department of Justice 1997).

Write policies clearly. Have a clear policy about serving children with special needs. Make sure it is written down and given to all parents, such as in the parent handbook. This keeps the decisions about placement and services from becoming personal for the families. It also gives parents the message that you are experienced in handling these issues.

Develop relationships. Start communicating with parents about their child's adjustment to school from the beginning. Waiting until things are overwhelming heightens tensions.

Discussion Questions

1. How were policies developed for your program? Do they stand the test of time, or are they based on people or situations that are no longer an issue?
2. What policies do parents seem to challenge the most? Do they make sense from the parents' perspective? What changes might encourage greater cooperation?
3. Is there common understanding between staff members about policies? What policies do you need to talk about as a staff?

Finding Common Values between Home and School

There is no such thing as a values-free program or curriculum. Values are at the heart of all the program and curriculum decisions we make. Sometimes our values are so ingrained in early childhood practices that we view them as facts, as what is simply good for children. We don't see that they are based on our beliefs until someone challenges them.

One of the critical roles of parents is to instill the values of their family, culture, and community in their children. This is easiest when children spend their lives in a community of like-minded people. But for many parents, it is impractical to restrict their children's experiences to interactions only with people of similar values. This is especially true for families who are not of the dominant culture. Many parents recognize the need for their children to succeed in the dominant culture, and they work to raise bicultural children: people who are at home in their own culture and in the culture of the dominant society. When parents make this choice, they must work hard to ensure that the values of their own culture are not lost.

Other parents may choose not to restrict their children's lives to like-minded people because they value multicultural experience. Parents often choose to send their children to nonsectarian schools even if programs that teach their faith are accessible. While parents may not have the right to expect a program to teach their values, they do have a right to expect a program to deal with differences in values in a respectful manner.

Differences in expectations for cleanliness, clothing, language, physical contact, and formality or informality in speaking to adults can all be examples of values-based conflicts:

Cleanliness. Parents have differing expectations regarding the cleanliness of their children and the environments to which they are exposed. Often these expectations are rooted in culture. Often teachers have a higher tolerance of dirt than parents.

Children's clothing. Some programs exclude party attire or clothing that has commercial messages, such as cartoon characters. Some programs insist that specific clothing is worn, such as closed-toed shoes to protect children's feet, shorts under dresses to protect girls' modesty, or underwear to protect children's hygiene.

Language. Programs may have rules about inappropriate language. This is a problem when families use words that aren't allowed as part of everyday speech, such as words for body parts (*butt*) or expressions (*Oh God!*).

Physical contact. A program may have rules that are too restrictive for a family to feel at home in (for example, not allowing children to kiss each other or adults, or not allowing children to sit on adults' laps). Or a program may have contact that is more demonstrative than some families prefer.

Adult-child relationships. Schools often direct children to call teachers either by their first names (informal), their last names (formal), or something in between, such as "Miss Kathy" or "Auntie." If families are uncomfortable with the titles, conflict can occur. Some families (often for cultural reasons) expect their children to address adults respectfully and insist that their child greet and respond to the teacher. A teacher may defend a child's refusal to acknowledge him as a way of putting parents at ease, but doing so may feel to parents like a lack of support for their family values.

Beginning with your initial contact with prospective families, you can take several steps to develop and communicate program values based on shared beliefs:

1. Focus on developing common ground.
2. Continue to develop shared understandings with new families as they enter your program.
3. Continue to focus on how decisions either support or compete with families' values throughout their experience with your program.

Focus on Developing Common Ground

You can begin by focusing on developing common ground regarding values. It begins with your first contact with prospective families.

First, acknowledge to yourself that you cannot develop a values-free program or curriculum. Be conscious of the decisions you make and which values you are supporting with those decisions. A preschool that offers only a part-day schedule projects a value about working parents. If this is not your intention, be clear about how you can meet the needs of working parents, and know that they will likely assume you do not value the choices they have made. A preschool that requires children to arrive by 9:00 a.m. projects a value about the schedules you expect families to keep. If this is not your intention, you may want to be flexible for parents who work evenings.

Second, make sure the information prospective families receive is detailed enough to allow them to determine if there is a good match between their values and the program's values. For example, parents can make informed choices if brochures or other materials make it clear that children are encouraged to get messy at school. For example, parents will not necessarily interpret pat phrases like "sensory-based experiences" or "discovery is encouraged" to mean that children may come home covered in paint.

And last, focus on the connection between program goals and curriculum decisions. Consistency in this area makes it easier for parents to predict issues that will come up. For instance, if a curriculum goal is to include families in their children's learning but you do not allow parents to assist in the classroom, your policies and goals are not in alignment.

Develop Shared Understandings with New Families

The next step is continuing to develop shared understandings with families as they enter your program. You can do this by spending time with families to learn about their values and discover potential conflicts and find solutions before their children begin. For instance, a teacher gave a tour of her program to a parent who commented that the bathrooms didn't seem very clean. Instead of simply reassuring her that they were cleaned twice per day (which is true), the teacher conducting the tour stopped and had a conversation about the program's value of independence (such as allowing children to change their own clothes, even if it meant clothing strewn across the room during the process) and the mother's feelings about independence and messiness. The family chose to enroll in the program and did so with full understanding of why the program operated certain ways rather than deciding just to tolerate a perceived flaw.

Listen to parents' beliefs and opinions with respect. You are more likely to pass judgment and view beliefs as eccentricities when they differ from your own. Taking time to truly hear what parents say may give you a new perspective.

Focus on How Decisions Support Families' Values

The third step involves continued focus on how decisions support or compete with families' values during their experience with your program. Remember the benefits of diversity. If you respond to disagreements by becoming annoyed or angry, you will miss opportunities to increase the diversity in your program. Uniformity may be easier, but it is much more boring!

Practice flexibility. Avoid reacting by saying, "We don't do it that way," and give yourself a chance to work with parents to invent a better way. One example is a family who came to a center I worked at from Japan. The mother wanted her child to wash her feet before meals and nap. Rather than just saying no, the teacher shared the challenges of doing so. The two of them finally came up with a plan to have the child use wipes to clean her own feet at these times. The parent felt supported, the child felt comfortable with a familiar routine, and the teacher established a positive beginning to their relationship.

When Nothing Seems to Work

There are times when a family's values will not mesh with the program. If you value diversity in your program, you should try to do what you can to find compromise. You may not be able to do so if one of the following could result:

The family disagrees with legally or ethically mandated practices. Our job is not to tell families how to discipline their children, but if we see evidence of abuse, we must report it. This will not necessarily result in the family leaving the program. In the past I have reported families for suspected abuse, and this did not lead to their pulling their children from the program. Still, you should be prepared for the possibility. You should also be certain to clearly review discipline policies as well as suspected abuse-reporting policies with each family during their initial orientation visit.

Meeting the family's expectations would result in a fundamental change in the program. We can expect families to roll with some changes, such as altering a lunch menu to accommodate a vegetarian family. But some changes are so dramatic that the program would cease to meet other families' expectations. For example, if the program focuses on teaching positive conflict resolution and a parent wants the teacher to allow his child to hit back, the values of the program would have to change significantly to comply. Still, it may be possible to start from a place of commonality (for example, "I know that you don't want Sam to get bullied at school, and I don't want that either") and make an agreement in which the parent's values and the school's values are both respected.

Ultimately, you must decide which values are worth alienating families for—or, as the saying goes, which mountains you are willing to die on. While it is hard not to view losing a family from your program as a failure, hanging on to a bad fit is like hanging on to a bad romance. You can grow as a professional when you consider other points of view, but ultimately you need to do what you believe is right. Be clear about what you are not willing to give up.

When Beliefs from Home and the Program Don't Match, or Holidaze

Maria shares her problem:

"This is my house! When Aaron's mom placed him, she told me they were Jewish. I thought that would be a nice change of pace for our group. I asked Aaron's mom to come in and light a menorah with the kids and tell us about their holiday. But now she doesn't want me to celebrate my holiday with the children! She complains about every decoration and Christmas-related book. It's not fair for her son's holiday to be the only one that is acknowledged."

Aaron's mom sees it differently:

"I knew that my son was going to be exposed to Christmas, and I'm fine with that. What I object to is that Christmas is the only theme for the whole month of December! One day for Hanukkah and thirty days for Christmas. Aaron is getting inundated with it. It's not just the commercial side of the holiday. She is reading stories about Jesus and has him singing religious carols. Now he wants to know why we can't have Christmas. She has Santa Claus coming to the house this week. I don't know what to do."

WHAT IS THE PROBLEM?

The issue surrounding holidays tends to be either about religious or cultural diversity or about commercialism. The diversity side of the issue involves supporting families' beliefs and values. While spending a day (or week) on each holiday seems fair to you, it is important to hear that it doesn't feel fair to the family who is not a part of majority American culture. When the experiences of a family do not match what is on television, in newspapers and magazines, and on display on every street corner, it is hard for them to enculturate their children. All American children, regardless of their religion or culture, become experts on Christmas, Easter, Halloween, and Thanksgiving. If children are raised in families that celebrate these holidays, it is easy for these children to be completely ignorant about other holidays and beliefs.

Holidays are especially tough for families who believe it is wrong for their families to celebrate them. For instance, some fundamentalist Christian families do not want their children exposed to Halloween, which they consider a pagan holiday. Jehovah's Witnesses may not celebrate any holidays or birthdays.

The other issue that comes up is commercialism. Even families who celebrate holidays may object to the focus on Madison Avenue and the "gimme" aspect of holidays. While these families might be pleased with a focus on family traditions, they may feel that Santa Claus, the Easter Bunny, and other nonreligious traditions undermine their family values.

WHAT ARE YOU THINKING?

Be aware of how your reaction might make the situation worse. Moving toward positive solutions is easier if you can recognize and avoid certain defensive mindsets that can make it difficult to develop a healthy partnership with parents. Typical defensive reactions include these:

"The parent is telling me what to do in my own classroom (or home or program)." You may become angry if you feel as if you are being bullied in your own environment. If you can push past this feeling to think about the immediate issue, your emotions won't run the show.

"The desires of the most demanding parents will overwhelm the rest." This can feel almost undemocratic. But resist resorting to majority rule, and find a solution everyone can live with.

"If the religious aspects of a holiday aren't allowed, we are trivializing something important and perpetuating commercialism." This again comes down to values. Focus on what really matters to you rather than creating a compromise that is unsatisfying to everyone involved, such as not including any of the holiday's religious parts.

SCENARIO 13

WHAT ARE PARENTS THINKING?

Thinking about how our actions strike emotional chords with parents (just as their actions have an impact on us) can help us to be more sensitive.

"The teacher thinks her values are more important than mine." This is especially challenging if your culture or religion has been marginalized in the past.

"My child is going to wish that we had a different religion." While we as adults may value exposure to a variety of cultures and religions, the younger the child, the more confusing this exposure can be. This is especially challenging for children who are seeing images of the majority religion in public.

SOLVING THE PROBLEM

Once a family objects to your focus on a holiday, you need to decide what you are willing to compromise.

Listen to the parent's feelings. This may be the most important step if this parent perceives that she hasn't been listened to before on this matter. Reflect back her feelings so she knows you truly heard her.

Share your feelings. Don't let your feelings get personal. These are emotional issues, and you can be firm without belittling different beliefs or traditions. "I understand this has made you uncomfortable. I didn't think about that. Christmas is such a joyous time in our family that I just wanted to share it with the children."

Find a compromise. Approach the family in a nondefensive manner, and figure out what you can both live with. Are there days the family is planning to be away? If so, this is a good time to concentrate on the activities they have the least comfort with. Maybe you can allow the family to take absence on those days without charging them. I taught a child whose mother had died the previous year. I met with his guardians, who had talked to a psychologist to make a plan to reduce the trauma of Mother's Day. We decided to save some stories and other activities for days when he would be absent, hoping he would not be as tender next year.

AFTER THE PROBLEM IS SOLVED: MOVING TOWARD TRUE PARTNERSHIP

You can address each issue as it comes up, or you can stretch yourself and your policies to partner with families. The following are places to start:

Create a plan with families. Involve parents in a focused discussion about celebrations so you won't be surprised by their reactions. You can talk as a group of parents and staff about shared values concerning traditions and celebrations. The group can write a position statement or another document that details what they want children to learn about their own family traditions, the beliefs and traditions of others, and common values and experiences. You can then refer to this document when making future holiday plans. While this may feel like giving up a lot of control, you are building support for your curriculum.

Create new celebrations for your program. You can enjoy all of the festivities of holidays without stepping on anyone's toes. Maybe you have major celebrations over losing a tooth or the birthday of a favorite author. For more suggestions about new school traditions, read Bonnie Neugebauer's article "Going One Step Further—No Traditional Holidays" (1994).

BEFORE YOU HAVE A PROBLEM

The following suggestions can be used to avoid problems with families who have concerns about holiday celebrations.

Focus on developing common ground. Acknowledge to yourself that you cannot develop a values-free curriculum. Explain what you will celebrate and why.

Develop shared understandings with new families as they enter your program. Make sure materials that go to prospective families have enough information so they can decide if the program is a good match with their values. When a child enters your program, be sure families understand your curriculum. Be as specific as possible about activities, plans, and alternatives. Put it in writing. Make sure to include a section in your parent handbook about holiday policies.

Focus on the connection between program goals and curriculum decisions. Make sure parents are prepared for each new event. Remind them ahead of time. Send out a note a month before a holiday explaining what you will do and why, and what you want from parents. If your program begins in the fall, Halloween

SCENARIO 13

tends to be the first big holiday to face. If you don't want masks, costumes, or candy, tell parents clearly and tell them why. Some examples: Masks are too scary for younger or sensitive children; costumes may tear and disappoint children or make children too excitable; you avoid sweets in your program and know children will already be getting a lot of candy elsewhere; you have so many interesting things to focus on in your program, and you don't think Halloween is worth the attention. Even if you have told them before, they may not have processed what you mean. "You mean my daughter can't even wear her costume? We weren't planning on trick-or-treating, so I only bought it for school."

SCENARIO

14

Controlling Pretend Play, or "Not my son!"

Monique feels challenged by this father's attitude:

"We offer a developmentally appropriate program here, and part of that includes supporting children's sociodramatic play. I find the children who spend a lot of time in the housekeeping corner to be the ones who need that play the most. Logan is a sweet little boy who loves to dress up. He comes in every day, puts on the same Cinderella-type gown, and then joins classroom activities. His mom is fine with it, but his dad is clearly uncomfortable. He makes fun of Logan and tells him he's acting like a sissy. We had our parent-teacher conference last week, and his dad told me he doesn't want me to let Logan dress up in girls' clothing anymore. I don't know what to do."

Larry is concerned:

"It's not like I'm afraid my son is gay, but I don't like it when he dresses up like a girl. This is the age when children are learning values. If we don't teach him what it means to be male, he might be confused. The teacher and my wife don't understand how tough it is to grow up male. Kids are not going to understand if he wants to wear dresses in kindergarten! I don't want my son to be teased or get beat up because he doesn't know how to be a boy. I am just trying to act now to avoid problems in the future."

WHAT IS THE PROBLEM?

Parents are naturally concerned that they will lose influence over their children when other adults play such a significant role in their lives. Parents do not want

SCENARIO 14

to make a mistake that will have a negative impact on their children. Some parents are surprised to find out how conservative their own values are once they are raising children.

WHAT ARE YOU THINKING?

Be aware of how your reaction might make the situation worse. Moving toward positive solutions is easier if you can recognize and avoid certain defensive mindsets that can make it difficult to develop a healthy partnership with parents. Typical defensive reactions include these:

"This parent is trying to impose his prejudices onto the classroom." Creating a values-free classroom isn't possible. Every choice you make, from the way you arrange the physical environment to the books you read and the hours you are open, reflects your values. When families are in agreement, these values become almost invisible. When families differ in opinion, values stick out and can be the source of conflict.

"If I take dress-up out of my classroom, then I have rewarded the squeaky wheel." You assume that families have chosen your program because of, in some part, common values. You don't want to give up something that is important to you and the other families. Rather than thinking of this as a power struggle with a winner and a loser, think of it as a highly emotional issue that requires careful consideration.

WHAT ARE PARENTS THINKING?

Thinking about how our actions strike emotional chords with parents (just as their actions have an impact on us) can help us to be more sensitive.

"The teachers don't understand how this can affect my child." Culture has a strong influence over gender expectations. Families are expected to prepare their children to become functioning members of their culture. When those cultural expectations are at odds with the culture of the school, it creates conflict. If it is important to you to have a multicultural program, you will need to come to terms with these issues.

SOLVING THE PROBLEM

This is not an unusual problem. You can find solutions through balancing the values of parents and your own values.

Hear the families' concerns. Families may have information about their lives that you are not aware of. Even if you don't agree in the end, hearing it will help you develop a relationship.

Explain why you think the activity is important for their child. Help families to see the behavior within the context of the child's current developmental stage. We know that most little boys who like to play dress-up don't grow up to be gay or transvestite, but parents don't have the breadth of experience we do. They may need reassuring. Remind parents that the fun of costumes is wearing what you would not otherwise wear.

Suggest a limited risk. Ask parents to give the child time to lose interest in the play. Most children who play constantly with one game or activity eventually finish and move on.

Find a supportive third person for the family. Ask the parent of an older child who has moved on from a similar stage of dressing up to talk to this family. Getting permission from both families before mentioning each to the other may be tricky, but having that conversation may be a valuable experience for both of them.

Work with the family to find common goals for the child. Most parents would not be attracted to our programs if they did not see some common ground. An example of seemingly opposite family preferences attracted to the same program is a preschool at a nature center, which attracted parents who were hunters and parents who were vegetarians. Both were interested in a program that included a nature component. The school and its parents found a comfort level on these topics when parents were able to share their differences and support each other's home values; later their children had lively discussions on the topic. The same can happen in programs with children from different religions. The most important value to reinforce is "That's what you do in your family."

AFTER THE PROBLEM IS SOLVED: MOVING TOWARD TRUE PARTNERSHIP

Rather than providing prepared costumes, some programs give children the materials to make their own dress-up outfits. Pieces of fabric, paper, scissors, tape, beads for making jewelry, and similar materials can bring out more creativity in children.

BEFORE YOU HAVE A PROBLEM

The following suggestions can be used to avoid problems with families whose values are different from your program values.

Focus on developing common ground. Acknowledge to yourself that you cannot develop a values-free curriculum. Put the program's goals and values in writing. This can be done in a brochure, on a website, or in another format. Being as open as possible helps parents decide if your program is a good fit for their family. If families know that creative self-expression and fantasy play are an important part of your program and that this means that children may play dress-up in clothes that are usually worn by the other gender, they may be better prepared.

Develop shared understandings with new families as they enter your program. Make sure materials for prospective families have enough information so they can decide if the program is a good match with their values. Give clear information about classroom activities before families enroll. Offering families tours of the school during free-play time will help them see typical activities. Give them a chance to ask questions after the tour.

Focus on the connection between program goals and curriculum decisions. Help parents see the connection between program goals and children's development. The connection between pretend play and development is not as clear to parents as it is to us. Take time during parent-teacher conferences, parent meetings, and in newsletters and other forms of communication to connect the dots for families.

Practice flexibility. Make sure you have inviting dress-up clothes that boys would wear, as well as dress-up clothes for girls. Too often teachers throw a few ties and men's shoes in the dress-up corner, and they are not particularly interesting for boys. Pay attention to what the boys in your program like to pretend, and have dress-up items for those roles. It may be costumes, camouflage, fishing vests, and so forth. If a child senses that his parents don't like him dressing up in girls' clothes, he is stuck either complying with their demands or feeling guilty when he does not. You can save him from this conflict by providing items that are glitzy and fancy and that lend themselves to fantasy play without being clearly for females. Some examples include the sequined vests of bullfighters, little tuxedo jackets, sports clothing, animal costumes, and kings' robes and crowns. Or create a dress-up collection that isn't gender specific. Robes, occupational costumes, and animal costumes will be less likely to make parents uncomfortable.

SCENARIO 15

Fear of Losing Influence over One's Own Child, or "Whose child is this, anyway?"

Tamara is annoyed:

"When the Smiths enrolled their daughter, Paige, in my program, they told me that they didn't have a television in their home and didn't want her watching TV. We agreed that if the other children were watching a video, I would give her an art activity in the kitchen. Paige's parents made it sound as if she would go along with it. Well, she won't. She feels left out when the other children are watching TV and she is made to stay out of the room. Now I feel guilty for having the television on. I find myself trying to talk the kids out of a video. Before Paige came, we had a nice routine of the older children having quiet time in front of a video while the little kids were napping. Now I find myself turning the whole house upside down to satisfy the parents' demands. Even though I don't let her watch the videos, her parents complain that she is picking up TV stuff, and they don't like it."

Mrs. Smith feels tricked:

"Raising our children according to our values is important to us. We don't like what television does to children. It makes them more violent and less compassionate. It also encourages commercialism. When we enrolled Paige in the family child care program, we noticed there was a TV, and we shared our concerns. Tamara told us the kids hardly ever watch TV and agreed to provide an alternative activity for Paige if the television was on. Well, 'hardly ever' turns out to mean every day! It's obvious that Tamara

resents having to come up with a different activity for Paige, so she just throws playdough on a table in the kitchen. She says Paige doesn't want to stay in the kitchen—who can blame her? We don't see why she can't just come up with something more positive than plopping the children in front of the TV. Tamara says she doesn't let Paige watch it, but Paige is coming home singing cartoon theme songs and whining for toys we have never told her about. She must be getting that from TV."

WHAT IS THE PROBLEM?

This issue is twofold. First, the parents have a different vision of what family child care should look like than the caregiver has. Second, they are concerned that they are losing control over their child's values.

Parents who choose to place their children in family child care may have different visions of what they hope their children will experience. For some, it is an experience close to what their child would have if they stayed home with them. These parents may appreciate the homelike touches of children eating at a kitchen table rather than a classroom table, playing in a living room or backyard, playing with children of a variety of ages, as they would experience in an extended family, and having a relaxed atmosphere that is more like home than an institutional school. For families with this vision, it may seem normal for children to watch television on occasion, as they might at home, or they might expect that TV would be avoided because of the smaller group size and more relaxed atmosphere. Others may view family child care as preschool on a smaller scale. They may expect a more school-like atmosphere, with more rigid schedules, structured activities, and "learning" as the primary goal of all activities during the day. For these parents, TV may seem inappropriate.

Further, some parents feel at constant war with media and other institutions for control of their children's values. They may resent the push for commercialism. They may dislike the exposure to violence, sex, or other themes they believe to be at odds with their own convictions. They may want to choose when to broach certain topics with their children rather than have their children receive information (or misinformation) from others.

WHAT ARE YOU THINKING?

Be aware of how your reaction might make the situation worse. Moving toward positive solutions is easier if you can recognize and avoid certain defensive mind-sets that can make it difficult to develop a healthy partnership with parents. Typical defensive reactions include these:

"This parent doesn't think I am doing a good job." Trying not to feel judged by parents' criticism is hard. Letting go of your defensiveness and listening to parents' concerns is more productive.

"The parent is trying to control what goes on in my house." When you open your house up to family child care, you turn your home into a business. You give up some of the privacy and control you had before.

"The parent is insisting on changes that ruin everything that's been working so well!" When a program is running smoothly, contemplating change becomes hard. Try to truly consider making changes so that your own fear of change doesn't keep you from evaluating the situation.

WHAT ARE PARENTS THINKING?

Thinking about how our actions strike emotional chords with parents (just as their actions have an impact on us) can help us to be more sensitive.

"The caregiver doesn't care what we want." "She is just going to do whatever is easiest for her, not what's right for my child." Being unable to control the influences on your child is a powerless feeling.

"I don't want my child exposed to this influence!" Are there religious issues for the families in your program? Some fundamentalist religions are especially concerned with the influence of television.

SOLVING THE PROBLEM

Once you discover that the parents' expectations do not match your plans, provide information to help everyone decide if this is the best placement.

Avoid getting defensive. The family's disagreement isn't about you, it's about their child.

Remember, the parents' role is as advocate for their child and family. Don't expect them to care about what the other parents or children want. Their focus is their own child. Your job is to watch out for the interests of the other families.

Make a plan with the parents that you can both live with. Put the plan in writing so both groups leave with the same version. Agree to revisit the issue at a later date.

AFTER THE PROBLEM IS SOLVED: MOVING TOWARD TRUE PARTNERSHIP

You can look at this problem as an opportunity to develop new strategies to partner with parents.

Invite the parents to send ideas. Have the parents suggest projects that would serve the same goal as watching TV—a quiet, restful activity for the children. Listening to audiobooks might be a good alternative.

Research professional journals. Research the effects of TV watching for children and recommendations from the field. The National Association for the Education of Young Children (NAEYC) and the American Academy of Pediatrics both have a position statement on passive media use, and you may want to learn the reasons that watching television is not recommended in early childhood programs.

Conduct a parent survey. See how the other parents in your program feel about the use of TV. More families may be concerned than you know.

BEFORE YOU HAVE A PROBLEM

The following suggestions can be used to avoid problems with families who have different ideas about the use of passive media.

Develop shared understandings with new families when they enter your program. Make sure materials for prospective families have enough information so they can decide if the program is a good match with their values. Give accurate information about your program before a family enrolls. Don't use terms like *occasionally* or *hardly ever*, because they may mean "once per week" to you and "once per year" to the parents. Provide a clear picture of what a typical day looks like, as well as a less-typical day. What do you do if it's raining? What do you do if one of your children is sick and separated in his bedroom? How do you treat special occasions? Be clear about your rules. Can children bring in videos to share? Which videos? Do you stay in the room with children who are watching television? Which network shows can children watch?

Focus on the connection between program goals and curriculum decisions. Be clear about your program's goals. You cannot be all things to all people. You have a limited number of families you can serve. Everyone will have a better experience if you are on the same page about what children are going to experience.

Spend time with families to learn about their values. Understand parents' expectations. Do they expect you to offer a unique activity for their child? Do they hope you will discourage watching television? How hard do they expect you to work to keep their child from catching a glimpse of TV? Do they expect you to limit pretend play that involves TV characters?

Separating Twins, or "Why can't my boys be together?"

Sonya is frustrated by a parent's resistance:

"I always have twins in separate classrooms. I have had a lot of twins in our school over the years, and I know they tend to stick together. One of the main reasons for sending your children to school is so they will make friends. If twins are in the same class, that won't happen. Twins also sometimes have delayed language because they are so used to communicating with each other. If they are going to develop their communication, they need to learn to communicate with other children."

Ms. Hernandez doesn't understand:

"My boys have always been together. I want them to go to school so they will learn, but they will be miserable if they are not together. Why is the teacher trying to make them go in separate classrooms? They won't be any trouble!"

WHAT IS THE PROBLEM?

Sonya is focused on her goals for the children. She wants children to make friends with other children. Sonya is basing her decision to separate the twins on her past experience. Ms. Hernandez knows best about her own children. Ms. Hernandez is committed to the relationship between her sons, and her goals for them at school differ from the teacher's goals.

WHAT ARE YOU THINKING?

Be aware of how your reaction might make the situation worse. Moving toward positive solutions is easier if you can recognize and avoid certain defensive mindsets that can make it difficult to develop a healthy partnership with parents. Typical defensive reactions include these:

"These boys will never make any friends if they are together." If this has been your experience in the past, you can actually inhibit friendship building by looking for problems where they may not exist.

"If their language is delayed, it will reflect badly on my teaching." With the high stakes involved in outcomes, it is challenging not to worry and make decisions for children based on our own need to prove ourselves.

"Sometimes twins egg each other on and get into trouble. It will be easier for the class if they aren't together." Teachers often do all they can to avoid challenging behavior, and if they think twins may misbehave together, the teacher's need for a challenge-free classroom may override the best interest of the twins.

"This mother needs to trust my knowledge." Remember that you may be the expert in child development, but parents are the experts on their own children.

WHAT ARE PARENTS THINKING?

Thinking about how our actions strike emotional chords with parents (just as their actions have an impact on us) can help us to be more sensitive.

"My boys will have to separate from both me and from each other. It's not fair!" It is natural for parents to worry about separation anxiety and adjustment to school. This mom has a legitimate concern about her sons experiencing twice the separation.

"My sons won't want to go to school." Even though we know that many children take time to adjust to school, if this mother has doubts about her sons' ability to adjust, they are more likely to find adjustment challenging.

"I should look for a school that will let them be together." If parents don't feel supported in their values for their children, they are likely to look elsewhere.

SOLVING THE PROBLEM

Once you realize what the mother wants for her boys, try to make a plan together.

Listen with an open mind to the parent's position on keeping her twins in the same class. She may provide useful information to help you evaluate if this is an issue. Do the boys have separate friends outside of school? Do they have experience in Sunday school or other settings? Do they tend to play with toys together or separately?

Share your experiences with twins in the past. Share your concerns without sounding like the expert. Ask the mother if what you've told her changes her mind about her wishes for her boys.

Consider starting the boys in the same class while they adjust to school and moving one to another class if problems come up. This communicates your understanding of the mother's wishes for her sons.

AFTER THE PROBLEM IS SOLVED: MOVING TOWARD TRUE PARTNERSHIP

Keeping an open mind cannot only help you to partner with this family but can also provide you with an opportunity for professional growth.

Research professional journals. Research the pros and cons of keeping twins in the same classroom. This is a common area of study, and you should be able to find useful information to guide your future plans.

Make plans with parents for placement of their twins. Rather than having a policy on whether twins should be placed together, meet with parents individually, share the data you have, ask questions about what they know about their own children, and make a plan accordingly.

BEFORE YOU HAVE A PROBLEM

The following suggestions can be used to avoid problems with families wanting more influence over their children's placements in classrooms.

Focus on developing common ground. Acknowledge to yourself that you cannot develop a values-free program. Share what your goals are for children's experience in school with their families and be open to their goals as well.

Discussion Questions

1. When you were growing up, was your family very much like the families of your schoolmates? How accepting were classmates and teachers of different families?

2. What values and beliefs are most central to your work with children? How are those reflected in your practices and policies?

3. If you currently work with children, how much diversity is there among your families? How have you accommodated their values and beliefs?

Child Development Issues

While various philosophies influence early childhood programs, early childhood professionals share common understandings about how children grow and learn. Parents don't have that luxury. While teachers can refer to research, parents are getting advice from in-laws, friends, and the latest articles in the press. What may seem clear to us may seem like a fad to parents. Spank or don't spank? Pacifiers? Academics- or play-based programs? We can change our minds about our style of teaching, but parents must live with the consequences of their mistakes. If we keep in mind the conflicting information and high stakes parents must contend with, it is easier to be patient when we disagree with them.

Talking to Parents about Stages of Development

One of the gifts we offer parents is information about typical child development. While parents know more than teachers about their own children, we have the broad knowledge that comes from spending time with many children of the same age. In addition, teachers have information about child development research from classes, reading, and professional development. Some conflicts between parents and teachers come from this difference in confidence about what is accurate in child development. While listening to what parents know about their children is important, we can also alleviate their concerns by sharing information with parents about stages of child development. Some of these issues include discipline, academics- versus play-based programs, toilet training, biting, lying, and other age-specific behaviors.

Discipline. Teachers tend to have clear ideas about what kind of discipline is appropriate for young children, and we are often quickest to judge parents about it. The most common complaint that teachers have about parents is lack of consistency when it comes to discipline. We need to remember that it is much easier to be consistent in school than it is at home. We have an environment that is exclusively (or almost exclusively) used for young children. We don't have dangerous or fragile objects around, as most homes do. We aren't trying to get other things done (such as cleaning or working) while we are with children. We are fresh (at least compared to parents, who may have just woken up, worked a ten-hour shift, or driven a long commute). At our best, we are doing something we were trained to do, and we are not personally embarrassed by the behavior of the children.

Before I was a mother, I would watch a child crying in a shopping cart and think, "What is that horrible parent doing to that poor child?" After I joined the parenthood club, I would react by thinking, "That poor mom!" Before you become frustrated with the parent who gives in to whining children, behaves inconsistently, or reacts negatively instead of taking positive action, think about how much more challenging it is to parent for life than it is to teach for eight or fewer hours per day.

Academics- versus play-based programs. Teachers have the support of organizations, such as the National Association for the Education of Young Children (NAEYC), to inform our opinions on what kind of education is best for young children. Parents are judged by everyone. They have the memories of their own schooling (and most people cannot remember their own preschool experiences, so they are really thinking back to first grade) and assume that what was exciting, scary, or difficult for them will seem that way to their children. Grandparents and other relatives are more than happy to share opinions. For every article about the Hurried Child, there is another telling them not to let their children be left behind. Knowing this, you shouldn't be surprised if parents aren't quick to trust that you know what form of education is best for their children.

Toilet training. Teachers have accepted practices that support children's toilet learning. Even our practices have changed a little recently because pediatricians are now saying later is better for many children (Choby and George 2008). Parents have much less experience in toilet training than we do (how many children does the average toddler teacher toilet train in her career?), less ideal circumstances in which to do it (we don't have children in restaurants, on vacation, on long car trips, or on the way to the grocery store), and less trust that it will all happen. We might say, "I've never sent a child off to college in diapers," but the parent is worried about kindergarten. Even our policies tend to send mixed messages to parents. Many preschool programs won't take children who are not toilet trained, and then we judge parents for trying to rush children out of diapers! If we understand why toilet training is so hard for parents, we can work more closely with them during the toilet-training stage and be more understanding when they are less than consistent.

Biting, lying, and other age-specific behaviors. Teachers know and see common behavior patterns in children's development. When children who do not have the language skills to communicate are frustrated, they are more likely to bite than older, more competent children are. We don't worry that toddlers who bite will grow up to be ax murderers, but parents don't have the experience of watching many children outgrow this behavior or the distance to not take it personally. Similarly, when young children do not tell the truth, we understand that fantasy versus reality is not fixed for them. Parents are thinking instead about their children's characters. They are understandably on the lookout for difficult personality traits that will negatively affect their children's lives, while they, as parents, still have a chance to help correct such flaws. If we understand how loaded these issues are for parents, we can give them good information about child development so they can view these behaviors with less concern.

Support Parents' Understanding of Their Children's Development

To work well with parents around discipline issues, keep the following ideas in mind:

1. Help parents see that development is dynamic.
2. Offer parents information about development and resources for learning more.
3. Share information with parents about child guidance.
4. Remember that there is more than one right way to work with children.
5. Support parents' choices.

Help Parents See That Development Is Dynamic

As a field, we have moved beyond the lockstep notions of what two-year-olds or three-year-olds are like that were established in the 1920s. We now understand that innate qualities, family life, culture, experience, and other factors all affect development. We will serve children and families better if we don't expect all children of the same chronological age to be on the same page. We can help parents focus on helping their children develop greater competency (such as learning to comfort themselves, tie their shoes, or read their names) rather than giving them the message that a child should already be doing these things.

Offer Parents Information about Development and Resources for Learning More

For many families, we are the primary avenue for their education. By taking this responsibility seriously and making information accessible, we help parents be their most competent. The side benefit for us is that parents who are more informed can support what we are doing in the classroom. We can share information formally by offering resources, such as lending libraries, child development information in parent newsletters, lectures on parenting, ideas for home activities, toy lending library, comprehensive parent-teacher conferences, and public programs for parents. Many parents find the most beneficial method of parent education to be casual conversations about what their children are doing and how that fits in the greater scheme of development. Another great avenue for teaching parents about development is by displaying their children's classroom work with explanatory messages.

Share Information with Parents about Child Guidance

Many parents find discipline challenging at one time or another. Most parents really appreciate having teachers they can talk to about struggles at home, including eating, sleeping, sibling rivalry, and other situations that don't come up at school. Rather than framing advice as "You should . . . ," you can make suggestions such as, "Some parents have been successful by. . . ."

Remember That There Is More Than One Correct Way to Work with Children

While it helps parents when we provide information about child guidance, teachers can step over the line into prescribing solutions that don't fit the families. In the end, parents need to make their own choices. You may be uncomfortable with a method like bribery, but it may fit the culture of the family.

Support the Choices Parents Make

Parents need our support. If they don't want children eating certain foods, we need to support them, even if we think it is silly. They don't need us judging their decisions. Most of them have plenty of relatives to do that for them!

When Nothing Seems to Work

Dealing with the learning curve some parents have when learning about child development is frustrating. Many teachers want parents to agree with their positions and accept their knowledge and opinions unconditionally, or they want the families out of the program. If we don't accept that parents have something to teach us and that they will sometimes be right (does that make us wrong?), we will miss great learning opportunities for ourselves. Even if differences in opinion are based on parents' misunderstandings about typical child development, we shouldn't give up on parents and our differences too fast. By helping parents become more competent, we will have an effect on children that lasts long beyond their years with us.

If you are considering asking a parent to find another program, ask yourself the following questions:

- Do the parents' actions in response to their child's development interfere with the safety and well-being of other children in the program?
- Even if this is true, is the child's behavior showing improvement?
- Can you maintain a positive relationship with the family even if they aren't on the same page with you on this issue?

Taking School Toys Home, or "My little Jesse James"

Joe doesn't understand why the parent got so agitated:

"I noticed some of our Matchbox cars were disappearing when I prepared the classroom before school each day. I started watching, and sure enough, Marty was slipping toy cars into his pocket during cleanup time. My coteacher and I had a chuckle. She talked to Marty's mom about it, and she agreed to check his pants when he got home. As he was leaving on Tuesday, I noticed a bulge in his pants pocket, so I stopped him and checked. I found a car and reminded him gently about leaving school toys at school. It was no big deal. That evening his mom called my coteacher at home and said I had humiliated her. She wanted me to apologize! I didn't accuse her of stealing!"

Marty's mom is seething:

"I was so embarrassed! Marty's teacher called him a thief right in front of all the other families! Marty is a little forgetful and probably just put the car in his pocket during cleanup and forgot it was there. Joe seems to have it out for him. He searched his pockets right there in front of everyone. I can't even talk to Joe anymore."

WHAT IS THE PROBLEM?

Two issues cloud this scenario: a parent's lack of insight into a developmental understanding of ownership and the way feedback about a child can feel personal to a parent.

One of the best pieces written on developmental understanding of ownership is "Toddler's Rules of Possession." (It appears, unattributed, on many websites. Just search for the title on the Web to read the whole list.) The author does an amusing job of portraying the wishful thinking ("If I saw it first, it's mine") of young children. As educators, we have vast experience with this thinking and don't view such actions as thievery. Parents are less likely to understand this, and any borrowing of toys can make a parent worry that they have a budding kleptomaniac on their hands.

The second issue of personalization also complicates this scenario. Parents identify so closely with their children that they can experience criticism of their child as criticism of themselves.

WHAT ARE YOU THINKING?

Be aware of how your reaction might make the situation worse. Moving toward positive solutions is easier if you can recognize and avoid certain defensive mindsets that can make it difficult to develop a healthy partnership with parents. Typical defensive reactions include these:

"This mom is deflecting her embarrassment by finding fault with my behavior!" This may be true, but it is human nature. If you can avoid embarrassing people, they don't have to defend themselves by attacking you.

"The mother is putting words in my mouth! I didn't say her son was a thief." This can be frustrating, but if you understand how parents hear your words, it will be easier to clear up the disagreement.

"The mother is enabling her son by focusing on what I did and not on what he did." A parent will naturally try to protect her child. Finding a way to express concerns delicately can avoid defensiveness.

"She just blew this all out of proportion. Before this, Marty and I had a great relationship, and now he thinks I don't like him." Try not to allow the problem between the adults to change your relationship with the child.

WHAT ARE PARENTS THINKING?

Thinking about how our actions strike emotional chords with parents (just as their actions have an impact on us) can help us to be more sensitive.

"The teacher accused my child of stealing!" You never know what experiences parents bring to adulthood. If parents have been unjustly accused of a misdeed in their own childhood, they are more likely to meet defensively a similar issue involving their children.

"What's the big deal? It's just a cheap car!" Different cultures have different attitudes about ownership. A parent may think that you have plenty of cars. It won't be a problem for her child to take one.

"Joe doesn't trust me to handle this." From the perspective of the parent, Joe asked her to deal with an issue and then didn't give her a chance to do so. From Joe's perspective, he was helping and supporting the parent by following through with the situation at hand.

SOLVING THE PROBLEM

Getting back into a trusting relationship with this parent will take some work.

Hear how the parent feels. Rather than starting to defend yourself, really listen to the parent about both what she thinks and what she feels. Use a reflective message to let her know you understand: "So you were planning on checking for toys when you had more privacy. When I brought it up in front of other families, it was embarrassing for you."

Explain why you did what you did. "I didn't realize it would feel that way to you. I thought if I was matter-of-fact about the whole thing, it wouldn't be a big deal."

Make sure the parent knows you have positive feelings for her child. "I know Marty didn't mean to steal it. At this age, children still think that wishing something were theirs has the power to make it so. I admire that Marty knows what he wants!"

Help the parent understand that the behavior is normal. Refer parents to a book, such as *Practical Solutions to Practically Every Problem* (Saifer 2016), to help put the issue in perspective.

Assure the parent that you will be more sensitive to confidentiality in the future. Parents have the right to privacy about the potential misdeeds of their children.

AFTER THE PROBLEM IS SOLVED: MOVING TOWARD TRUE PARTNERSHIP

You can look at this problem as an opportunity to develop new strategies to support both parents and children at different stages of development.

Let children borrow books and toys from school. Allowing families to borrow toys and books from the program to bring home minimizes their desire to take without asking and is a great way to experience sharing.

Provide a box for children to drop toys they have "accidently" put in pockets or taken home. This allows families to deal with this without the embarrassment of teacher involvement.

BEFORE YOU HAVE A PROBLEM

The following suggestions can be used to avoid problems when children take school items home.

Offer parents information about development and resources for learning more. Your parent library can be full of books on development issues. Copy a page on issues common to this age group, such as "taking what isn't yours," and post it on your parent bulletin board or in class newsletters.

Model examining issues from the child's perspective. If parents see us asking questions to learn why children behave in certain ways (maybe the child has a toy just like it at home), then they will not feel as judged or embarrassed when an issue comes up.

SCENARIO

The Parent Who Personalizes Her Child's Rejection, or "Then you can't come to my birthday party."

Pam describes her frustration:

"Four-year-olds are experimenting with friendship. They proclaim best friends, get in fights, hate each other, and are best friends again before lunch. It is no big deal until the parents get involved. Olivia's mom takes it so seriously. She heard that one of the other children was having a party and didn't invite Olivia. She showed up in tears and didn't want me to let the children talk about it at school. She called the parents of the other little girls and cried about how much Olivia was devastated by the whole thing. Olivia doesn't seem devastated. She still plays with the other child. The mom of the birthday girl came to me so embarrassed. She doesn't want to have all of the kids over for a party, and I think that is her right. But the bad feelings are taking over the whole school. Parents are talking in the parking lot. I don't know what to do!"

Olivia's mom explains how she feels:

"It's just so hurtful. Olivia just loves this little girl Beth. Beth is one of those power-hungry little girls who acts like the queen of the class. She is having this big party and never misses an opportunity to point out to Olivia that she isn't coming. I could just slap Beth's smug little face. I tried appealing to her mother about how important this is for Olivia, but she is just like her daughter. Her teacher doesn't understand how hard this is on Olivia. If they are all so unfeeling, maybe she'd be better off in another school."

WHAT IS THE PROBLEM?

Parents bring to the classroom all of their own history and baggage. It is not unusual for this to show up when parents react to a rejection or other negative experience as if it is happening to them instead. Expecting a parent to be logical will not help you. Appealing to a parent's sense of proportion is also unlikely to be successful. If you do not acknowledge the parent's feelings and help them move on, you are likely to encounter this issue again.

WHAT ARE YOU THINKING?

Be aware of how your reaction might make the situation worse. Moving toward positive solutions is easier if you can recognize and avoid certain defensive mindsets that can make it difficult to develop a healthy partnership with parents. Typical defensive reactions include these:

"This parent is crazy." It is reasonable to be cautious about your involvement with unbalanced parents, but it is more helpful to begin with the assumption that this is a blind spot in an otherwise normal person.

"I am getting dragged into issues that are not in my job description." Your first focus should be on the children, and it is important that you do not allow the drama of the adults to become your focus. It is also true that the emotions of parents follow their children into the school. If you ignore them, you lose the opportunity to keep them from getting out of control.

"This parent is turning her child into a princess." Watching a parent miss an opportunity to teach her child resiliency is difficult. You cannot change a parent's basic beliefs, but you can model other ways of interaction.

WHAT ARE PARENTS THINKING?

Thinking about how our actions strike emotional chords with parents (just as their actions have an impact on us) can help us to be more sensitive.

"This school teaches children to be self-centered." In some cultures, the good of the whole group takes precedence over the good of the individual. I had a Japanese parent confront me on my ethnocentric policies that placed priority on the individual's right to choose playmates (or implicitly to exclude others) over the well-being of the whole class. It made an impression on me because it was her child who was doing the excluding, and she didn't want me to allow him to do so.

"This is an insult to all of us." Saving face for the family is an issue in some cultures, and a slight to the child is a slight to the whole family. In many cultures, an egocentric parent isn't the only one who takes such actions personally. Including everyone in social events is a basis for community harmony. If this is the case, you can take the role of "cultural translator" and help the other parent see why this is an issue.

"I have failed my daughter. I have not taught her how to make friends." If the parent's cultural identity is largely set by her role as a mother, it will be harder for her to separate herself from her child. I mentored an international program in which nonworking mothers in foreign countries were placed in the difficult position where their husbands' corporate expectations were to place the children in a full-day program. These mothers were torn between supporting their husbands' careers by placing their children with the other expatriate children and their need to be with their children in a place where they otherwise knew nobody. The program wisely created many activities and reasons for mothers to spend a large part of the day helping in the library, office, and other parts of the program without interfering with their children's adjustment to school.

SOLVING THE PROBLEM

Once the problem has started, you can take the teachable moment to help the parent differentiate between herself and her child.

Hear and reflect your understanding of the parent's pain. Reassure the parent that you will be sensitive to emotional undercurrents at school. "It must be so hard to think that your child is getting rejected. I don't want children to have that experience, and I keep an eye on how children treat each other at school."

Help the parent understand the typical social world of children of this age. "What I have seen is that at this age, children are best friends on the playground, mad at each other during snack, and forget all about it by nap."

Suggest to the mom that she try to stay neutral. Staying neutral makes it easier for friendships to mend when this event has been forgotten. "If you resist giving it attention, it will be easier for Olivia to regain her friendship with Beth."

Help parents see this as an opportunity to develop resilience in their children. "If Olivia can learn to ignore children when they behave this way, she will innoculate herself against peer pressure." While watching this process, Olivia's mom may become more resilient herself.

Avoid getting dragged into the dispute. Be very careful not to take sides with one parent or to say or do anything that can be viewed as taking sides. When one person is in conflict with another person, gathering allies is natural. Refuse to say anything about the other parent, even if you have information that might help the conflicted parent understand the situation better. For example, it's not your place to say, "She has a small house and couldn't fit more children in it for a party."

Offer stories to help parents develop perspective. Using examples of your own experiences to illustrate a point can be helpful. "When my son was that age, another child said something mean to him and it upset me so much, I didn't even want to see the other boy's mom. The children were over it in a few days. My job was to put my feelings aside and be happy for my son's closure on the whole thing."

Don't let the dispute follow the families into the program. Pretend you don't know anything about it. Don't arrange for members of the families to stay away from each other in school or make other allowances for the event.

Don't allow adults to make negative statements about other families or children in your presence. If you see a cluster of parents gossiping, nicely but firmly ask them to take it outdoors.

AFTER THE PROBLEM IS SOLVED: MOVING TOWARD TRUE PARTNERSHIP

You can look at this problem as an opportunity to develop new strategies to support both parents and children at different stages of development.

Help parents connect. Part of creating a sense of community in the classroom includes creating community between families. If parents come to know each other well in the context of school, behavior that hurts feelings may be less likely to take place. Classroom involvement, PTA-type organizations, and parent education classes are all opportunities for families to get to know each other.

Offer parenting classes. Parenting classes can offer adults the chance to deal with their own issues when they come up within the context of parenting. In one parenting class in a Minnesota community, parents read Vivian Paley's *You Can't Say You Can't Play* (1993), which deals with exclusion and ways to create a rejection-free zone in your classroom. Parents who read this book dealt with their own experiences growing up and were able to differentiate between their experiences and those of their children with greater ease.

BEFORE YOU HAVE A PROBLEM

The following suggestions can be used to avoid problems with parents who personalize their children's social struggles.

Offer parents information about development and resources for learning more. Parents may not think about the ramifications of including some classmates and excluding others. Set the parameters for the intersections between family and school life. In this particular case, steps could have been taken not to allow invitations to be passed out at school. And Olivia's mom could use information about friendship patterns for children at this age.

Share information with parents about child guidance. Give parents guidance in beginning their children's social lives outside of school. One common rule of thumb is allowing one invitee for each year the child has achieved. This means that a three-year-old would invite only three friends.

Support parents' choices. You can help parents stay out of this predicament by providing celebrations at school. While some schools do not want social events to take over the program, this can be especially appropriate in family child care settings.

The New School Year, or "Where are my daughter's friends?"

Shannon feels hassled by this parent's complaints:

"We put a lot of time and energy into placing children in classes for the new school year. The teachers for the two-year-old rooms help us divide up the kids who are going to the three-year-old rooms. We told Tanya's mother she was going to be in my class this year, and she seemed happy about it. Now it's the third day of school and she wants Tanya moved to the other class for threes. She says all of Tanya's friends are in there and Tanya doesn't want to come to school anymore. Mom thinks it's a problem that we didn't put Tanya in the same class as her friend Erica. We intentionally placed them in different classes. We want Tanya to show more independence—she did everything Erica told her to. Why can't Tanya's mom understand this is for her own good?"

Tanya's mom is surprised by her daughter's tears:

"I wasn't prepared for Tanya to have such a hard time settling into school this year. Last year we knew it would be tough. She was only two, and we spent a long time helping her through the transition. Now she knows this school and the routines and seemed like she was really happy to come to the big class. We didn't realize none of her friends would be with her. I can't take another year of her crying about school. If they would just move her, I know it would be okay."

SCENARIO 19

WHAT IS THE PROBLEM?

Watching their child go from loving school to not wanting to go can be devastating for parents. Parents often ask children why they don't like school, and most children don't have the ability to verbalize their gut feelings. They try to express their unhappiness, and parents leap to fix the problem. Teachers have the experience to know that a resistant child will likely settle in if the program has been successful for the child in the past. They want parents to show patience in the adjustment process, while parents are focused on wanting their child to be happy now.

WHAT ARE YOU THINKING?

Be aware of how your reaction might make the situation worse. Moving toward positive solutions is easier if you can recognize and avoid certain defensive mindsets that can make it difficult to develop a healthy partnership with parents. Typical defensive reactions include these:

"This parent is asking to pull her child out of my class! Doesn't she think I'm a good teacher?" Don't take this personally; the parent is focused on what she can do to make her child come to school willingly. Your becoming defensive may damage your relationship with this family.

"Doesn't this mom have any confidence in her daughter's ability to make new friends?" Parents often are insecure about their children's social abilities. This can be especially true if a parent had issues in this area growing up. She isn't going to be convinced otherwise by your words. She needs to experience her child's social competence.

"This mom wants us all to jump through hoops to give her daughter her way. How are we supposed to make room in that class for another child?" Remember, the parent is not focused on what is fair for other children; she is trying to advocate for her own child's needs. You will get further by helping the parent see how sticking with a placement will benefit her child rather than by appealing to a sense of fair play.

WHAT ARE PARENTS THINKING?

Thinking about how our actions strike emotional chords with parents (just as their actions have an impact on us) can help us to be more sensitive.

"The teachers don't understand how my child feels!" It is hard for parents to see teachers looking so matter-of-fact when their children are miserable. If parents are from a different culture than the teacher, there may be a difference in accepted ways to express feelings. Ask others if you look sympathetic when you feel that way. In some cultures, people cry easily; others are more stoic. You might work to match the needs of the parent.

"Why was my child placed in the less desirable classroom?" Sometimes parents get the mistaken (or sometimes accurate) impression that coveted placements with the favorite teacher or classroom go to favored families. If this is not the case, help parents understand how the placement process works.

"What happened to make my daughter unhappy at school?" Parents naturally look for a reason why a child who previously came to school willingly starts to resist. Even if parents have built a trusting relationship with last year's teacher, they are starting fresh with you.

SOLVING THE PROBLEM

Help parents move beyond their desire for a quick fix by helping them work through the transition.

Listen to parents' concerns. Use language to let them know you hear them and understand how they feel. Don't try to defend the placement decision. "You were really surprised when Tanya had another rough transition. It sounds like you expected that was all behind you. Tanya says she is sad because she isn't with her friends."

Share information about how placement decisions were made. "We wanted Tanya to be in this class because we thought it would be a good match for her. My teaching assistant plays the Autoharp, and we know how much Tanya loves music. We thought she would enjoy playing with some of the children who weren't in her class last year."

Let the parent know how Tanya is doing at school while acknowledging her experience. "After you leave, Tanya cries for a few minutes. She is willing to sit in my lap and accepts comfort from me. Yesterday I asked her if she wanted to draw a picture for you, which really made her feel better. I'm glad you told me how she is feeling so I know she needs a little more support in making friends."

Tell the parent what you expect. The parent only knows what her child is experiencing right now. "I have seen other children go through a few weeks of missing their old class and old friends. I expect that in a couple of weeks she will be very comfortable and won't long for the other class."

Tell the parent what steps you will take to help her child make the transition. Parents can be reassured when a concrete plan is in place.

Let the parent know how she can help. "If you can learn the names of the other children in our class, you can ask Tanya about them. I don't recommend asking if they are her friends, or she may feel pressured to create instant friends. If you ask her, 'What did Alice wear today?' or 'What did Antonio bring for lunch?' she will have a reason to pay attention to the other children, which is the first step toward friendship."

Tell the parent how her child will benefit from staying in your class. "I'm afraid if we move Tanya to the other class now, she will miss the opportunity to make a comfortable transition to a new class. She will have lots of changes throughout her life, and we can support her in building confidence while she's in preschool. I really feel that she will be happy in this class once she's made the adjustment."

Ask the parent to give it time to work. If a month from now the child is still miserable, more may be going on.

Communicate often with the parent during the transition period. Simple e-mails, texts, or phone calls let the parent know that you are still thinking about Tanya's needs.

AFTER THE PROBLEM IS SOLVED: MOVING TOWARD TRUE PARTNERSHIP

How do you involve families in the enrollment process? Even if you don't want to let it turn into a popularity contest, you can ask parents what they think their children need in a classroom or in a teacher. Learn this information by using questionnaires or having personal conversations.

BEFORE YOU HAVE A PROBLEM

The following suggestions can be used to avoid problems with parents who are concerned about their child's classmates.

Offer parents information about development and resources for learning more. Prepare parents for the beginning of a new year and for potential problems adjusting. We tend to give this issue a lot of energy when children first enter a program and forget that it may continue to be an issue in later years.

Share information with parents about child guidance. Give parents tips for preparing their child for a new class. If rosters are available beforehand, let parents know who will be in the same class with their child so they can work on making those connections as soon as possible.

Remember that there is more than one right way to work with children. Listen to what parents tell you about their child's friendship patterns. Just because it may work for you most of the time to move children into new groups, maybe parents know something that could help you make that decision.

SCENARIO

20

The Child Who Can Do No Wrong, or "Not my baby!"

Nicky's teacher paints a picture:

"Nicky is one of those kids I always have to keep an eye on. He doesn't have a lot of impulse control. He pinches other kids or knocks them over, and then looks innocent. I tried to talk to his mom about it. She just can't accept that he isn't an angel. She makes excuses for him or insists that I must have missed what the other child did to him first. She is making his behavior worse!"

Nicky's mom says:

"I don't think Nicky's teacher likes him. She is always blaming him for things. He's just a little boy! Sometimes when he really likes another child, he is a little too affectionate and doesn't know his own strength. He really is sweet."

WHAT IS THE PROBLEM?

Acknowledging their children's misbehavior can be difficult for parents. One reason for this is that parents' expectations of child behavior are not keeping up with their child's development. When parents learn to care for their newborn, they are told that their child isn't crying to get attention; the baby is letting his needs be known. As children move from unintentional actions to intentional actions, parents may not make the transition. This child's social development isn't age appropriate, and his mom is not aware of that.

WHAT ARE YOU THINKING?

Be aware of how your reaction might make the situation worse. Moving toward positive solutions is easier if you can recognize and avoid certain defensive mind-sets that can make it difficult to develop a healthy partnership with parents. Typical defensive reactions include these:

"The parents are spoiling that child!" Watching parents miss opportunities to teach their children responsibility can be hard, but teachers have no control over this. While we can provide insight to parents who are ready to hear it, we must ultimately let go.

"Other children and parents will lose respect for my authority if I can't get this child to behave." Your ego is not what counts in these situations. What is good for children is what matters. Rise above your concern for appearance and do what you know is right.

WHAT ARE PARENTS THINKING?

Thinking about how our actions strike emotional chords with parents (just as their actions have an impact on us) can help us to be more sensitive.

"She doesn't understand my son." Parents will accept most things if they believe you truly know their child and will act on his behalf.

"He is just a little child. What does the teacher expect?" Expectations vary by culture. Some cultures give children more time to not be responsible for their behavior.

"What does the teacher expect? He's all boy." A secondary issue is that in some cultures, expectations for boys are different from expectations for girls. If you know this to be the case, you can frame the behavioral expectations for the child in terms of what will be expected of him by his peers and grade school teachers rather than making it a gender issue.

SOLVING THE PROBLEM

The best way to help the child change his behavior is to work with parents on a consistent message and reaction to misbehaviors.

Give the parent honest information about her child. You may be tempted to pretend that the child is behaving fine at school and to handle the issue without involving parents. However, unless you have reason to believe that sharing information with the parent will place the child at risk for abuse, you must give the parent accurate information. The parent may not be ready to hear it from you, but this child's kindergarten teacher may get through to her, and the parent will realize the child's behavior has been an issue all along.

Be prepared for a negative reaction from the parent. Avoid a negative reaction by offering concrete examples of the behavior you are addressing. Saying, "Nicky reached over to another child and took the cookie cutter out of his hand while the other child was yelling 'no'" is specific. Saying, "Nicky always takes the other kids' toys" is not.

Don't get defensive. If the parent questions your judgment or the reliability of your observations, remember how defensive the parent feels and don't take it personally. Assume that the parent is also interested in seeing the child's behavior improve.

Work with the assumption that you and the parent have the same ultimate goal. You can make a parent defensive by asking if she allows her child to behave in a certain way. By starting off with the assumption that you have the same goal, you can establish that you're on a team with the parent.

Act with integrity. Don't talk about other children. If the parent baits you with observations about other children, firmly remind her that it is inappropriate to talk about other children. The purpose of the talk is to deal with her child.

Get help. If tensions are high, get an administrator to help you talk to the parent. I have watched parents bully staff who wanted to avoid confrontation into allowing unacceptable behavior from their children. A third party can keep the conversation on topic.

Find common goals and actions you can both agree on. Focus on the behavior goal for the child, not the needs of the other children in the class. A parent will appreciate your desire to help her child learn prosocial behavior.

Meet the parent on her turf. If you can interest a parent in working with you to change the child's behavior, give her the time and support for consistency between home and school. A home visit can provide insight for you and can let the child know that expectations will be consistent between home and school.

Involve the parent in the solution. One approach is to keep a behavior log that goes between home and school.

AFTER THE PROBLEM IS SOLVED: MOVING TOWARD TRUE PARTNERSHIP

Rather than predetermining behavioral expectations, you can build them with the parents in the program. A parent meeting before school starts for the year can be a time to set goals and expectations that everyone accepts.

BEFORE YOU HAVE A PROBLEM

The following suggestions can be used to avoid problems with parents whose expectations for their child's behavior are out of step with child development.

Keep in mind that development is dynamic. Children's development and behavior is influenced by the expectations of the adults who care for them. Establish your fondness for the child before addressing behavioral issues. Parents will find it easier to listen to criticism from someone who cares.

Offer parents information about development and resources for learning more. If parents have the opportunity to learn about reasonable expectations for their child at different ages, it will improve their parenting.

Invite the parent to observe the classroom. Sometimes parents will see behavior without having it pointed out.

Share information with parents about child guidance. Have in writing a clear policy for discipline. Make sure parents understand it before school begins.

Discussion Questions

1. Did your parents have reasonable expectations of you as a child? Which of their expectations now seem inappropriate? Did they base their expectations on the advice of others (such as family members), their own memories of childhood, or "expert" advice from books, magazines, or parenting classes?
2. With what age of children do you feel most comfortable? What is it you like about this age? What abilities or behaviors do you want to avoid by not working with children of another age group?
3. Have you moved from working with one age group to another? If so, what surprised you about what the new age group could or couldn't do?

Involving Your Director to Work Well with Families

Part of your team for working well with parents should include your director or administrator. When you work together, you can ensure that you are developing positive relationships, communicating effectively, supporting policies, and teaching parents about child development.

Differences in Perspective

Understanding the differing perspectives of early childhood education (ECE) directors is useful. Much of this book has been focused on the differences in perspectives of parents and teachers. Directors have their own perspectives. The following table offers some comparisons of the same issue from the perspective of parents, teachers, and directors.

Teacher	***Parent***	***Director***
My class: Teachers look at the needs of the whole group. *Example: I choose lunch menus that most of the children like.*	My kid: Parents are most focused on what their own child needs. *Example: My child hates apple juice. Why can't they serve orange juice?*	My program: A director balances the needs of the program constituents. *Example: Most kids like apple juice and it costs less than orange juice.*

Teacher	***Parent***	***Director***
The child is an individual: Teachers do not take the behavior of a child personally. *Example: I understand that a toddler is just "going through a stage" when he bites.*	The child is a reflection of me: When my child is criticized, I feel criticized too. *Example: People think I am a bad mother because my child bites.*	The child is a reflection of the classroom: Children's behavior gives information about the classroom climate. *Example: A biting toddler is a sign that something must change in the classroom.*
The culture of classroom: Teachers may talk about "the way we do things at Rainbow School" or "in the Bear Room." *Example: I expect children to come to school in "play clothes" that can get dirty.*	The culture of this specific family: Expectations for the child are based on many factors, including the culture of the family, which may differ in values from the school. *Example: I send my child to school in good clothes to demonstrate respect.*	A personal vision of the program: A director may vary certain practices that he or she feels personify the program. *Example: We're proud of our open school. We don't use bibs on toddlers because bibs don't look like an open school.*
What works for this child for the rest of the year: Teachers focus on what benefits the children during the time they are in a teaching group. The future is somewhat abstract. *Example: I encourage children to express negative feelings.*	What works for this child for the rest of his life: Parents have to think about who a child is going to be as an adult. *Example: I'm concerned that my child will be viewed as demanding or whiny in elementary school.*	What is going to make for an easy transition between classes: Directors are interested in minimizing difficulties when children move from one classroom to another. *Example: Children may be allowed to yell in one class, but yelling may not be tolerated in the next group, so I'd prefer to stay consistent.*
Security of the ECE knowledge base: Teachers know that they have standards of practice to rely on. *Example: I and my fellow teachers have support from multiple sources for allowing children to use invented spelling as they develop literacy skills.*	Insecurity of parents: Parents have a double bind: the importance of their work and the lack of unity regarding what the "good parent" does. *Example: I worry that this approach will encourage bad spelling and work against my child in kindergarten.*	Insecurity about enrollment patterns if popular opinion changes: Directors can feel pressured to provide assurance for unsure parents. *Example: I might ask a teacher to acquiesce to a parent's expectations about using more traditional literacy activities.*

As you can see from these examples, parents, teachers, and directors look at the same issue through different lenses. By understanding a director's perspective, you can more readily appreciate what the director brings to the table. And you will be less likely to feel unsupported when the director disagrees with you and be more open to learning from the director's perspective.

Suggestions for working with your director to benefit relationships with parents:

Keep your director informed. You may be tempted to avoid sharing negative information before you know if it will turn out to be a problem, but keeping your director in the loop will prepare her or him if the parent comes to talk.

Ask your director for advice. When you have challenges to your work with parents, the director can provide a useful perspective.

Invite parents to talk to the director. If you let parents know that you don't feel as if they are going behind your back when they speak to the director, they may be willing to share information with you that they have avoided telling you. It also gives parents the message that you are all a team.

Involving the Director: Relationships

Directors can assist teachers in developing relationships with parents, a topic explored in chapter 1. Before a family even enters a program, the director can share information about you as a teacher with the family that you might feel too shy to share yourself. Doing so can start those relationships off on the right foot.

A mother describes how this happened:

> *"When I heard that Kiki was being placed in Sarah's classroom, I wasn't too sure about it. Sarah is really young and kind of strange looking. She has pink streaks in her hair and tattoos. That isn't the way I picture a teacher looking. But the director gave me lots of information about Sarah without my even asking. She told me that Sarah looks young but she is actually in her thirties. She told me about Sarah's education. She also said she had placed Kiki in Sarah's classroom because Sarah is a musician, and she remembered me saying that Kiki's dad is in the symphony. Getting that information before I even met Sarah put my mind at ease, and we are off to a great start."*

When you are struggling with your relationship with a parent, your director can help you see the perspective of the parent, think through solutions, and provide opportunities for improvement. A teacher describes:

> *"I couldn't connect with Jarod's parents. They just didn't seem to like me. I talked to my director, Wayne, about it, and he pointed out that they pick up Jarod during circle time, so I never have time to talk to them. He offered to take over my circle so that I would be available when Jarod's parents came. I met them at the door and had a great story to tell them about what Jarod had done that day at the carpentry table. It was amazing! They told me about how he builds with his grandfather, and we talked for twenty minutes! Now we have such an easygoing relationship!"*

Involving the Director: Communicating with Parents

Your director can be a big help with communication. As described in chapter 2, talking to a colleague can help you to prepare for difficult conversations with parents. Your director can also provide coaching for these conversations. It is often helpful to ask the director to join you if you are talking about a conflict with parents. Jeff describes:

> *"I have been dreading talking to Melanie's parents about the way she teases the other children. I know her parents think she walks on water, and this isn't going to be easy. But I need to tell them how she is making the other children feel. I talked to my director about it, and she helped me plan what I am going to say in a way that Melanie's parents can hear. Now I am not so nervous."*

Sometimes it is helpful to include your director when you have had a conflict with parents. The director can bridge the competing perspectives. Keep in mind that your director can help by assisting both parties in communication rather than taking a side. It works best to include the director when both parents attend or the parent has an ally so that the meeting doesn't feel like an ambush. It will not help you in your relationship with a parent if he feels bullied. A parent describes:

> *"Joan and I were so mad at Tommy's teacher! When we had our parent-teacher conference, she was full of negative things to say*

about Tommy's academic skills. We felt that if he wasn't learning, she wasn't teaching him! We told Pam, the director, that we were pulling Tommy out of the school. Pam asked if she could meet with all of us together. We weren't sure about it, thinking that she would just take the teacher's side. Instead, she helped the teacher do a better job of explaining the Early Learning Standards to us and what the teacher was doing to help Tommy learn. We are much more comfortable now."

Involving the Director: Helping Parents Understand Policies

Chapter 3 describes how policies have a large impact on your relationship with parents. Some policies are always at the discretion of the teacher, and other policies are ones that only the director can address. Involving the director in helping parents understand policies will support your relationship with parents. A teacher describes how a director helped:

"Elaine's dad was so annoyed with me. He wanted his fourteen-year-old daughter to pick up Elaine on her way home from school. I explained that to keep children safe it was against our policy to let a child be signed out by anyone other than an adult. He yelled at me that Elaine's sister was more responsible than most adults and that it was unfair for us to expect him to leave work just to pick her up and drive her the block to their house. I asked the director to join us in the conversation, and the director talked about liability issues. Elaine's dad understood, and now we are okay. It never would have occurred to me to frame the concern in that way, but now I understand that it felt less personal to him."

You may also want to involve the director in discussions with families around policy issues so that the director understands when school policies have a negative impact on families. Rita describes:

"We have a policy in our school that no outside food is allowed. This is to ensure that no substances that children might be allergic to are introduced to the program. This was a big problem for Billy's parents. Our food is provided by a company that doesn't use organic or GMO-free foods. Billy's parents want him to eat what

they think is healthy. I understand their position. I asked the director to come to talk to us about it, and he said they could bring Billy's food with a guarantee that they wouldn't provide anything with peanuts. Now everyone is happy!"

Involving the Director: Values Issues

The role that values play in your relationship with parents is discussed in chapter 4. Communicating that we don't agree with parents' values, even if it is done unintentionally, is always detrimental. Directors can help mitigate differences in a positive manner. Betsy describes:

"We have a 'no weapon play' rule at our school. It is an important value of mine and part of why I wanted to work here. Robbie's parents are hunters and think it is ridiculous. I have reminded them of the rule, yet I still keep finding toy guns in his backpack. I told my director that I was going to share an article with Robbie's parents about the detrimental effects of weapon play on young children. She helped me understand how offensive that would be. She helped me figure out how instead to say that other families are expecting none of this kind of play at school and I would not be following policy if I allowed it. I am also letting them know that I will not make negative comments about guns in our class so they can feel like I am not ignoring their family values."

Involving the Director: Child Development Issues

Chapter 5 considers how understanding child development has a large impact on your relationship with parents. Your director has the advantage of knowing child development from the perspective of all age groups in your program and can help you frame conversations with parents around these issues. If you are working with parents of oldest or only children, they haven't had the benefit of seeing how children change over time and knowing what is reasonable to expect of their child's development. You may think that a parent's expectations are off and that their expectations may be more appropriate for the stage of development the child just completed. When issues regarding child development come up, talk to your director to get another perspective.

Amber describes:

> *"TJ has diabetes. His parents are understandably hypervigilant about his diet. But he is only three years old and doesn't really get it. We had a Halloween party after school, and TJ and his parents came and brought sugar-free treats for him. They had their backs to him, and TJ's little friend Sammy handed him a piece of candy. TJ's dad turned and saw it and screamed in front of all of the parents, "Oh my God! That kid is trying to kill TJ!" TJ dropped the candy. I just froze! I didn't know what to say. My director rushed to TJ's parents, put her arms around them, and said, "You must be so scared! It is so hard to worry about your son and have him out of your control when he is at school!" They both started to cry. She comforted them and then reassured them that this would never happen during the school day and that this situation was good practice for them to learn how to handle parties. She explained that three-year-old Sammy doesn't understand such dangers and that Sammy was trying to be a good friend. She also shared how important it is for TJ's friends not to view him as a ill child but just as TJ, and what that approach will mean for his self-concept. TJ's parents went to Sammy's parents to apologize, Sammy's parents apologized for Sammy's actions, and by the time it was over, they had a playdate planned. I could never have hoped for such a positive outcome!"*

Special Challenges

Working with your program director involves some specific challenges. The following are some issues and ideas for making the situation work for everyone involved.

The Teacher-Director

A teacher-director has to wear two hats—a director hat and a teacher hat. Teacher-directors may experience less support than other teachers because they don't usually have another administrator backing them up. I spent many years as a teacher-director and found a few groups to provide support for me when dealing with the challenge of working with parents. The team of teachers I worked with were a great support in sharing their experiences and offering me ideas. I always had advisory committees in my program made up of current parents, former parents, community members, and early childhood experts. These folks always had my back, and when I was off-base with families, they let me know. I also had a board of directors, school board members, executive directors, and college deans to make final decisions. One of the benefits of being a teacher-director is that parents tend to love their teachers and save their frustration with school policies or procedures for the director. As a teacher-director, I did not receive the grief that some directors do from parents.

Teacher-directors benefit most from the support of these groups when they are proactive with information to support groups who need to know. You will build trust when your support groups are prepared for issues they may have to deal with. A teacher-director shares her story:

> *"I had an incident with a parent regarding the use of the word* partner *rather than* wife *when we played Farmer in the Dell. I explained to the father that we had children in our program with same-sex parents and we wanted to be inclusive. The father seemed to accept the explanation, but later one of our teachers overheard the father on a call-in radio show describing the incident. I made sure to call the president of our board to inform her about what happened. She was very appreciative. The issue didn't come up again until parent-teacher conferences. The father explained that he was irritated by the situation because it "smacked of political correctness." The teaching assistant explained that we had children with many types of families, including a child who had lost both parents and was the ward of cousins. When it was explained in that manner, the father really got it. I felt so supported by both my board member president and teaching assistant! We really are a team!"*

The Absent Director

Some teachers are totally on their own. This may happen if you teach for a big agency or chain and the director is responsible for multiple sites. Sometimes these directors are so overwhelmed that they are involved only when there is a major problem. Overwhelmed directors may take the path of least resistance and just try to give either the teacher or the parent her way without taking time to work out a compromise.

You can make the best of this situation by finding out what form of communication your director prefers. Maybe you want to meet with him or her on a regular basis in person and give updates of parents, curriculum, and so forth. Perhaps your director prefers written reports, e-mails, or phone calls. Just like communicating with parents, consistent communication benefits the relationship you have with your director. If your director knows you stay on top of things, don't overreact, and only ask for help when you need it, you are more likely to get the support you need when problems with parents come up.

Handling Conflict with Your Director When Working with Parents

Disagreement between a teacher and director on how to handle a situation with parents is not uncommon. The following are strategies for dealing appropriately with these type of conflicts:

- Be clear about your disagreement. Read chapter 2 on communication, and avoid pitfalls by using positive strategies, such as the principles of respectful communication.
- Provide specific examples. Blanket statements like "You didn't support me with Mrs. Jones" will not be helpful. Give specific examples, such as, "When you told Mrs. Jones she could bring Tyler when it wasn't his school day after I had told her no, I felt unsupported."
- Listen to the perspective of the director. You may be tempted to listen in a manner that is just building your own defense. Instead, really listen, and you may find out there is less of a conflict than you thought.
- Have an idea for a solution. A real solution should go beyond the director just giving you your way. If a solution isn't easy for you two to find, agree to meet again.
- Finish with appreciation for the process. You will keep communication open in the future by verbalizing how the process has been beneficial.

When Nothing Seems to Work

Sometimes a difference in attitudes regarding working with parents cannot be bridged. Some conflicts may require you to find another place to work. Examples may include the following:

When you cannot trust the ethics of the director in relation to parents. For example, the director breaches families' confidentiality with an outside party.

When the actions of the director have the potential to make you legally liable. For example, the director lies to parents about what has happened in your classroom (for example, if a child is a victim of sexual bullying by another child) and requires you to do the same. Another example is a director who refuses to follow temporary restraining orders (TROs). This is a legal document that keeps certain individuals from coming into contact with others and is often related to domestic abuse.

When the director is actively sabotaging your relationships with families. For example, the director makes disparaging comments about you to families.

When your values for working with parents are too different from those of the director for you to follow school policy and keep your integrity intact. For example, a director refuses to allow you to communicate concern with a parent about her child's development.

If you are planning to leave a program because of such issues, make sure to do so in an ethical manner. Share concerns with the director rather than going over the director's head. Be open to the director suggesting an improvement in the situation. Lastly, do not share negative information about the director in other settings.

SCENARIO 21

Not Really Toilet Trained, or "Oops! Not again!"

Lisa, a teacher of three-year-olds, isn't sure what to do:

"The school rule is that children must be toilet trained to enroll. I have a new child, Molly, in my class. She is having accidents daily. I love Molly and don't want her kicked out of the school, because she is doing so well in other areas. I know I should tell the director, but I hope if I keep working on it, Molly will toilet train soon. I really don't mind dealing with her accidents, but I am noticing that it gives me less time for the other children in the class. I talk to her mom about it every day, and she just looks worried and says it doesn't happen at home. That seems hard to believe."

Molly's mom says:

"I am really happy with Molly's school, but they don't seem to be handling her toileting well. She comes home with wet pants every day. We don't have these issues at home. I know when she is going to need to go, and I take her to the bathroom. I only put diapers on her at nap and nighttime. I am worried they are going to kick her out. I love her teacher, but I wish she would be more responsible about taking Molly to the bathroom."

The director shares her perspective:

"I have an interview with all parents before they can enroll their children to make sure they understand our policies. One of those policies is we require toilet training. We aren't licensed for children in diapers, and we don't have teacher-child ratios that will accommodate a teacher leaving the group to change a child's clothes all the time. I appreciate what a

great relationship Lisa has with Molly's mom, but I have to focus on the bigger picture."

WHAT IS THE PROBLEM?

The problem is the intersection of what we know about child development and the needs of programs to meet licensing rules and stay financially sound. This program is not set up for children who are not toilet trained. They don't have a diapering station, ratios and group sizes that accommodate diapering, or a license for children in diapers (this often requires additional sinks and so forth). However, researchers have found that more children in the United States are completing toilet training later (Choby and George 2008), and that only 40–60 percent of children are toilet trained by the time they are three years old (Blum, Taubman, and Nemeth 2004).

WHAT ARE YOU THINKING?

Be aware of how your reaction might make the situation worse. Moving toward positive solutions is easier if you can recognize and avoid certain defensive mindsets that can make it difficult to develop a healthy partnership with parents. Typical defensive reactions include these:

"I wish this parent would tell the truth!" The parent may be telling the truth about the lack of accidents at home. Parents are sometimes so in tune to their children's biological rhythms that they don't even realize they are anticipating their child's toileting needs. Children are also better able to pay attention to their own toileting needs when they aren't distracted by school experiences.

"It isn't fair that I have to choose between ratting out the family or breaking school policy." You are part of a school community, and viewing administration in an adversarial manner does not help families. When you choose to work in a program, you must support its policies or work to change them. (More information on this topic can be found in the National Association for the Education of Young Children (NAEYC) "Code of Ethical Conduct.")

WHAT ARE PARENTS THINKING?

Thinking about how our actions strike emotional chords with parents (just as their actions have an impact on us) can help us to be more sensitive.

"This program is more concerned with their needs than with the needs of my child." Expecting parents to be more focused on budgetary and licensing issues than on what they want for their children isn't reasonable.

"Something is wrong with this teacher if she can't get my child to the bathroom." Unless parents have spent a lot of time volunteering or observing in a classroom, they don't have a sense of the constant demands on a teacher's time.

"I can't let them know that she is in diapers at nap and nighttime, or they will kick her out." The stakes are high for honesty when it means risking your child's placement in a school.

WHAT IS THE DIRECTOR THINKING?

The director has a different perspective.

"This parent wasn't honest with me at the enrollment conference." Directors usually work hard to ensure successful classes for both families and teachers. A misunderstanding like this can have a negative impact on the relationship between the director and the family.

"I turned down several other families to let this child in! Now I am going to be left with an opening in the class." Directors of tuition-based programs have the burden of ensuring that tuition brings in needed revenue. For this issue not to have an impact on decisions regarding disenrolling children from the program is unlikely.

"I need to protect the needs of the teacher and the other children in the class." While directors appreciate the positive relationships between parents and teachers, their job is to protect teachers from unreasonable workloads.

SOLVING THE PROBLEM

To solve this problem, each person involved will need to brainstorm, compromise, and exercise respect for the others.

The best approach is to all sit down together to make a plan. If you meet separately, keeping everyone's perspectives in mind will be more difficult.

Invite the parents to invite a spouse, relative, or friend to join the discussion. Making sure the parent does not feel ganged up on is important.

Have the director take the role of facilitator. While it is challenging for the director not to focus on his or her own needs, conflict resolution works best with a facilitator to make sure that everyone is heard, everyone can brainstorm ideas, and everyone agrees to a course of action. The director can step out of the role of facilitator to provide information that others may not know, such as licensing rules.

Begin by demonstrating that you understand the perspective of the parent. If you start off sharing the problem from your perspective, everyone will be defensive.

Make sure the parent knows you have positive feelings for her child. "I really love having Molly in my class, and I want us to figure out a way to keep her in our program!"

Avoid giving the impression that you don't believe what the parent has told you about her child's toilet training. Instead, provide information about how toileting at school is different from toileting at home. Children who consistently use the toilet at home sometimes are less consistent at school. They have more distractions, more activities they don't want to stop to use the bathroom, and the challenge of using a potty different from the one they are used to at home.

After the parent feels heard, share the challenges of a child having accidents in the classroom. "With so many children to work with, it can take me a while to notice that a child has wet her pants. I hate for her to sit in wet underwear. I also worry that she will become discouraged."

Brainstorm ideas to solve the problem. Is it possible for Molly to come in the morning and leave before nap while she is adjusting to toileting at school? Can an extra staff member be temporarily brought into the classroom to support Molly by taking her to the bathroom more often? Can the program hold the place for the child while her mother works on consistent toilet training? If the program cannot afford to do so, can the parent afford to pay tuition to hold the place?

Write a plan and make it available to all. All participants will feel more secure if they are assured that everyone is leaving the meeting with the same understanding.

AFTER THE PROBLEM IS SOLVED: MOVING TOWARD TRUE PARTNERSHIP

You can look at this problem as an opportunity to develop new strategies to support both parents and children at different stages of development.

Develop a system for providing the parent daily information about toileting success. Focusing on what went well rather than on accidents will be best for the child, parent, and school. "Today Molly was playing in the water table and stopped to say, 'Oh, I have to pee!' Water play often makes children need to urinate, and it is a huge step for Molly to recognize this sensation and to be willing to leave a favorite activity to take care of it!"

Provide information for all parents with suggestions for toilet training. This can be done by handing out articles at enrollment or offering web links on the school's homepage.

BEFORE YOU HAVE A PROBLEM

The following suggestions can be used to avoid problems with parents around toileting issues.

Talk to your director about rethinking the toilet training policy. Even programs that accept children who are two and a half years old often require toilet training, which is inconsistent with current child development information. Programs like "Potty Boot Camp" are springing up around the country for desperate parents trying to make their children eligible for preschool. These programs may use harsh methods to ensure toilet training because they are paid for successful toilet training regardless of a child's readiness. In 2015 a woman running one of these programs was found guilty of child assault for holding a child on the toilet with enough firmness to leave bruises (Fugimoto). Is it possible to add a changing station to classrooms for three-year-olds? This is especially important for children with special needs. Keep in mind that even private programs are required to meet the requirements of the Americans with Disabilities Act (ADA), and this may mean enrolling children who are not toilet trained.

Make a plan for children with variable ability to control bladder and bowel to enter the program successfully. If parents know they can work with you, you may not have problems after enrollment. Strategies include gradual entry, short days, allowing use of diapers for a period of time, and bringing in extra staff temporarily.

SCENARIO 22

SCENARIO 22

When a Child Reports an Event to Parents Incorrectly, or "I want to talk to the parents about what really happened!"

Kala is really distressed:

"I just found out that one of the parents is mad at me. Her daughter, Maya, has a hard time settling down for nap. We let the children look at books until the resting music comes on, and then the children have to put their books away. Maya takes so long to settle down that I always let her go a little longer. The child who rests next to Maya, Caitlin, is more belligerent. One day Caitlin kept running around the room, not making her bed, and singing loudly. When the music came on, Caitlin got out a book. I told her it was too late and she couldn't look at a book. Caitlin pouted but eventually went to sleep. I didn't think anything more of it. Later that day, I got a text from the director telling me that Maya had told her parents that I punished her and wouldn't let her look at a book. I explained to the director that I stopped Caitlin, not Maya, from looking at a book. Maya was not punished, so I don't know why she told her parents this, and I said that I wanted to talk to Maya's parents. The director said I shouldn't talk to them, I should just let it drop. The next day, Maya was moved to the other class for naptime. I felt like I was being punished! Now Maya doesn't play with me anymore, and I feel like this whole thing has been a mess. I am ready to quit my job!"

Maya's mom says:

"Maya has a hard time napping at school. They seem to understand this and have made allowances for her. She came home from school the other

day and said she didn't want to go back to school. She told us that Kala had punished her for taking too long to settle down and wouldn't let her look at a book. I called the director, and she said she would take care of it. They moved Maya to the other room for nap, and she is fine now."

The director shares her perspective:

"Kala is a good teacher, but she can be a little inflexible when it comes to rules. Maya is a sensitive child and her parents were a little worried about how she would do in preschool. We made arrangements for Maya to take a little more time to settle in to nap and everything seemed to be fine. I got a call from Maya's mother telling me that Kala wasn't following our agreement regarding Maya getting more time. I texted Kala to tell her about it, and she explained that it wasn't Maya that she had disciplined but the child resting next to her. It makes sense that a child as sensitive as Maya would personalize the experience. Kala wanted to talk to the parent about it, but it seemed like it would blow the whole thing out of perspective, so I told her not to. We just moved Maya to the other resting room, and everything is fine now."

WHAT IS THE PROBLEM?

The real problem here is a lack of mutual trust on the part of the parent, the teacher, and the director. The parent doesn't trust the teacher to be sensitive to her child. The teacher doesn't trust the director to have her back with the parent. The director doesn't trust the teacher to respond sensitively to the parent.

WHAT ARE YOU THINKING?

Be aware of how your reaction might make the situation worse. Moving toward positive solutions is easier if you can recognize and avoid certain defensive mindsets that can make it difficult to develop a healthy partnership with parents. Typical defensive reactions include these:

"The parent is taking her child's word over mine." Because they are not there to see for themselves, parents are often concerned about what happens at school. The fact that the parent contacted the director shows that she was looking for more information rather than just allowing her child to stop attending school.

"The parent and the director have undermined my relationship with Maya." There are many possible reasons for a child to stop playing with a teacher after a conflict such as this. It could be that she is picking up on the teacher's wariness.

"The director is taking sides with the parent." Without a conversation with the director about why she didn't want Kala to talk to the parent, it may seem as if the director is taking sides. She may just be trying to defuse the tension.

"The director doesn't respect me." It is devastating to feel disrespected by your supervisor. This is why direct communication is so important.

WHAT ARE PARENTS THINKING?

Thinking about how our actions strike emotional chords with parents (just as their actions have an impact on us) can help us to be more sensitive.

"I can't stand having my daughter unhappy at school." Many parents have mixed feelings about having their young children in care. When a child who has gone to school happily for a long time suddenly resists going, it can be concerning for a parent.

"They think I coddle my daughter too much." Parents of sensitive children become more aware of their children's difference when their children enter school and there are other children to compare them to. Sometimes they assume judgment by others.

"What else has happened at school that I don't know about?" Parents feel anxious when they do not know what is going on when their children are in care.

WHAT IS THE DIRECTOR THINKING?

The director has a different perspective.

"We have worked hard to make this program work for this family, and the last thing I need is Kala undermining the work." Directors have the responsibility to enroll children, set policy, make needed exceptions to policies, and supervise the actions of teachers. The director is understandably focused more on the needs of the family than on the needs of the teacher, even though the teacher has no other source of support.

"The best thing I can do is to solve this problem quickly so it won't become a bigger problem." The director may be right that quick action will defuse the situation. However, it is possible that taking action without focusing on better communication will have unintended consequences that will make things much worse.

"Kala is making this about her feelings rather than the feelings of the child and the parent." The director is forgetting that she has a responsibility to care for Kala's feelings.

SOLVING THE PROBLEM

A lot has happened that will make solving this problem challenging, but it can be done without the program losing either the family or the teacher.

The director needs to meet with the teacher. Without taking the time to find out what really happened and how the teacher feels, the situation will only get worse.

Set a meeting for the parent, teacher, and director. The director should take the role of facilitator and assist in communication.

The teacher should practice what she will say to the parent. Role-playing with another staff member would be helpful. During the role play, the director can watch and help the teacher see when she is being defensive or not communicating clearly.

Take care to avoid breaching confidentiality. In a situation like this, slipping into talking about Caitlin or other children would be easy.

AFTER THE PROBLEM IS SOLVED: MOVING TOWARD TRUE PARTNERSHIP

This problem can be the catalyst for improving communication for all parties.

Plan home visits with Maya's family. This will help rebuild relationships.

Set times for extended meetings between the director and the teacher. Waiting for a problem before having conversations creates additional problems.

BEFORE YOU HAVE A PROBLEM

The following suggestions can be used to avoid communication problems.

Include teachers in intake interviews with parents. Confusion can be created when directors and parents make plans together without including teachers.

SCENARIO 22

Teachers may not have a full understanding of the agreements and the reasons behind them. Directors and parents may not be aware of possible negative consequences for the decisions they have made.

Plan consistent communication between parents and teachers. See chapter 2 for more information on communicating with families.

Directors should speak to teachers to get their understanding of events before speaking to parents. A director can say to the family, "Let me see what I can find out, and I will get back to you."

Discussion Questions

1. Think about your own leadership style. How do you lead and support families, teaching assistants, and other individuals you work with and are responsible for? Is it similar to the leadership style of your director? If not, how can you bridge the differences so you can make best use of what your director has to offer?
2. As you read through this chapter, what ideas can help you work with your director to build positive relationships with parents? Set at least one goal for new strategies.
3. Would you like to have more leadership responsibility someday? If so, how can this chapter inform your work with staff in their relationships with families?

Checklist for Analyzing Scenarios

Use this checklist to think about your own challenges working with parents.

Creating positive relationships

- ○ Take time to develop lasting relationships with parents.
- ○ Be available.
- ○ Be yourself.
- ○ Share while staying within your own personal boundaries.
- ○ Be trustworthy.
- ○ Remember that the relationship is in service to the child, not your needs.

Communicating with parents

- ○ Let parents lead the conversation.
- ○ Be proactive with information.
- ○ Focus on the parents' perspectives.
- ○ Plan for addressing problems with parents.
- ○ Take time to respond thoughtfully to parents' comments and requests.
- ○ Use the principles of active listening and respectful communication.
- ○ Give parents the benefit of the doubt.

Working with parents around policies

- ○ Write policies clearly.
- ○ Give parents copies of policies.
- ○ Talk to parents about policies during enrollment.
- ○ Compromise and stay flexible whenever possible.
- ○ Avoid judgments about parents' concerns or disagreements with policies.
- ○ Understand parents' concern for their child's happiness.

Working with parents around values issues

- ○ Spend time with families to learn about their values.
- ○ Develop shared understandings with new families as they enter your program.
- ○ Focus on developing common ground.
- ○ Focus on the connection between program goals and curriculum decisions.
- ○ Practice flexibility.

Working with parents around child development issues

- ○ Help parents see that development is dynamic.
- ○ Offer parents information about development and resources for learning more.
- ○ Share information with parents about child guidance.
- ○ Remember that there is more than one right way to work with children.
- ○ Support parents' choices.

References and Recommended Readings

References

Balaban, Nancy. 1985. *Starting School: From Separation to Independence: A Guide for Early Childhood Teachers.* New York: Teachers College Press.

Blum, Nathan J., Bruce Taubman, and Nicole Nemeth. 2004. "Why Is Toilet Training Occurring at Older Ages? A Study of Factors Associated with Later Training." *Journal of Pediatrics* 145 (1): 107–11.

Choby, Beth A. and Shefaa George. 2008. "Toilet Training." *American Family Physician* 78 (9): 1059–64.

Fugimoto, Lila. 2015. "Toddler had new bruises after first day at potty boot camp." *Maui News.*

Galinsky, Ellen. 1987. *The Six Stages of Parenthood.* New York: Perseus Books.

Katz, Lilian. 1995. "The Use of NAEYC's Code of Ethical Conduct within Child Care Facilities." Presentation at the NAEYC Annual Conference, Washington, DC.

NAEYC. 2011. "Code of Ethical Conduct and Statement of Commitment." www.naeyc.org/files/naeyc/image/public_policy/Ethics%20Position %20Statement2011_09202013update.pdf.

Neugebauer, Bonnie. 1994. "Going One Step Further—No Traditional Holidays." *Child Care Information Exchange.*

Paley, Vivian Gussin. 1993. *You Can't Say You Can't Play.* Cambridge, MA: Howard University Press.

Saifer, Steffen. 2016. *Practical Solutions to Practically Every Problem: The Survival Guide for Early Childhood Professionals,* 25th Anniversary Edition. St. Paul: Redleaf Press.

U.S. Department of Justice. 1997. *Commonly Asked Questions about Child Care Centers and the Americans with Disabilities Act.* www.ada.gov/childqanda.htm.

Recommended Readings

Gonzales-Mena, Janet. 1995. *Dragon Mom: Confessions of a Child Development Expert.* Napa, CA: Rattle OK Publications.

Honig, Alice Sterling. 2002. *Secure Relationships: Nurturing Infant/Toddler Attachment in Early Care Settings.* Washington, DC: NAEYC.

McCracken, Janet Brown. 1997. "So Many Goodbyes." Washington, DC: NAEYC.

Neugebauer, Bonnie. 1992. *Alike and Different: Exploring Our Humanity with Young Children.* Washington, DC: NAEYC.

Stonehouse, Anne. 1995. *How Does It Feel? Child Care from a Parent's Perspective.* Redmond, WA: Exchange Press.